T0129334

AMERICAN HEROES

AMERICAN HEROES

FASCINATING FACTS AND INSPIRING VOICES

MARTIN FEESS

AMERICAN HEROES
FASCINATING FACTS AND INSPIRING VOICES

iUniverse books may be ordered through booksellers or by contacting:

iUniverse
1663 Liberty Drive
Bloomington, IN 47403
www.iuniverse.com
1-800-Authors (1-800-288-4677)

ISBN: 978-1-5320-5216-3 (sc)
ISBN: 978-1-5320-5215-6 (e)

Library of Congress Control Number: 2018906837

Print information available on the last page.

iUniverse rev. date: 06/20/2018

CONTENTS

PART 1

FORMING A NATION

P ride in America is not misplaced. The United States was the world's first modern democracy[1], and it is evolving toward the ideals of "liberty and equality." However, if we are to be honest about the process of colonization and transformation to the American nation as we know it today, we must admit that the rights of indigenous people were ignored, and many were forced from their land, while Africans were abducted from their homeland, enslaved, degraded, and subjected to inhumane treatment. Grave crimes were committed toward members of both of these groups. These are facts that, though uncomfortable, must be acknowledged by all Americans if they are to understand each other and themselves. As inheritors of the fruits of the past, we all have a certain responsibility to help with the repair. There is, of course, another side to early US history, a story of nobility, courage, and leadership that propelled a young nation forward. Let us strive to understand this period of history in its complexity and derive useful lessons from it.

---

[1] Technically the United States is a federal republic, not a pure democracy.

CHAPTER 1

ENGLISH COLONIZATION OF AMERICA, 1607-1763

The first successful English colony in North America was the Jamestown Colony which was established in 1607.[2] This was a business venture inspired by the Spanish colonies that had produced significant amounts of gold. The Jamestown colonists discovered no gold and suffered severe hardships due to their failure to plant crops and build houses while hunting for gold. Many colonists died. The colony was saved when John Smith took charge with a simple rule: Those who do not work will not eat. The colony became successful because the colonists learned to grow and use tobacco from the indigenous local people. The leading tobacco grower was John Rolfe, who married the now famous Pocahontas. The marriage cemented an alliance between the English and the most powerful local indigenous tribe.

Tobacco growing proved to be somewhat labor intensive. Workers were needed. To fill this need, the growers of the new colony began acquiring black African slaves in 1619. By that time, the colony had expanded into the Virginia Colony.[3] Other southern colonies, which were established after, also grew tobacco and used slave labor.

Much farther north the Pilgrims established the Plymouth Colony in 1620. These Pilgrim were part of a larger religious group called Puritans. They wanted to "purify" the Church of England—to make it more about God and less about ritual and ornamentation. These colonists also

---

[2] "Jamestown" was named after King James I, the English king at that time.

[3] "Virginia" was named after the great Queen Elizabeth, who had never married and was subsequently dubbed "the Virgin Queen."

struggled considerably and were helped by local indigenous people who taught them how to plant crops and survive. In 1630 the Pilgrims were joined by larger group of Puritans and the Massachusetts Colony was established. The Puritans found lots of vacant land. Indigenous people in the region had lived in small villages and their numbers were not great to begin with. Then in the early 1600s plagues of European diseases struck this region. Indigenous folks had no immunity built up to these strange diseases. The death toll was catastrophic. The very religious Puritans misinterpreted this as a sign from God. He had cleared this land for them, they thought. As the Massachusetts Colony expanded, many colonists moved aggressively into the interior of the continent. A pattern was established which continued until the end of the nineteenth century. White settlers moved westward to possess land to which they felt entitled, and they pushed indigenous people further to the west. White civilization had the advantages of greater technology, greater numbers, and devastating disease.

The reasons for establishing colonies and the ways in which colonies were formed varied considerably. Three colonizers stand out among all others for their decency, humanity, and vision of equality: (1) Roger Williams of Rhode Island, (2) William Penn of Pennsylvania, and (3) James Oglethorpe of Georgia. One colonial citizen, Benjamin Franklin, stands out as widely accomplished.

Roger Williams (1603-1683) and Rhode Island

(1) Roger Williams had been ordained as a minister in 1631, the year he migrated to Massachusetts from England. This was only one year after the first large migration of Puritans to the colony.

(2) Williams ran into conflict with the Puritan leaders of Massachusetts over a number of issues, chiefly his belief that every person should be free to follow his own conscience in choosing a religion, or even choosing no religion.

(3) Williams contended that the English colonists had no right to any land in America without purchasing the land from the indigenous occupants.

(4) In 1635 Williams was convicted of sedition[4] and heresy[5] and banished from Massachusetts. This is when he established his Providence colony.

(5) In 1636 Roger Williams established the Providence Colony on land he had purchased from the local indigenous people. That colony grew to be the colony of Rhode Island.

(6) Williams had a gift for languages. He knew several European languages and learned some indigenous American language.

(7) Rhode Island became the only English-American colony to officially allow complete religious freedom to all, including non-Christians and atheists.

(8) Rhode Island became a haven for religious dissenters, including the free thinking Anne Hutchinson. Puritan leaders in Massachusetts objected to her teachings and to the fact that she was a female preacher. In Massachusetts, men only were allowed to lead religious study.

(9) Under Roger Williams, Rhode Island maintained friendly relations with the neighboring indigenous Narragansetts tribe for forty years.

(10) Williams published the first Anglo-American study of indigenous American language and culture, *Key into the Language of America.*

(11) Roger Williams believed that baptism required informed consent, and he founded the First Baptist Church in America.

(12) Rhode Island was the first English-American colony to establish the principal of separation of church and state. No European country had done this either.

Quotes from Roger Williams

God requireth not a uniformity of religion.

The greatest crime is not developing your potential. When you do what you do best, you help, not only yourself, but the whole world.

---

[4] "Sedition" is an attempt to stir rebellion against the government.

[5] "Heresy" religious teaching which is considered to be false.

It is less hurtful to compel a man to marry someone whom he does not love than to follow a religion in which he does not believe.

God is too large to be housed under one roof.

The sovereign power of all civil authority is founded in the consent of the governed.

Forced worship stinks in God's nostrils.

That cannot be a true religion which needs carnal[6] weapons to uphold it.

William Penn (1644-1718) and Pennsylvania

(1) William Penn was a member of the Society of Friends (Quakers), a Christian Protestant religious sect in England which forbade fighting (including war) and practiced total equality. Because they believed all people to be equal, Quakers refused to address the king by his royal rank.

(2) William Penn's father, an admiral in the British navy, beat young William in an attempt to get him to renounce his Quaker beliefs. When that didn't work, the admiral expelled his rebellious son from the family home.

(3) In 1668, Penn was imprisoned in the Tower of London for 8 months for some of his religious writings. During that time he refused to make any retraction.

(4) Admiral Sir William Penn, the father, was granted a charter for land in the New World by King Charles II. William Penn, the son, established the colony.

(5) Penn's colony was named Pennsylvania (Penn's woods).

(6) William Penn had legal title to the land under English law, but he still purchased part of "his land" from an indigenous tribe that had been living there.

---

[6] Carnal: material or worldly.

(7) Pennsylvania, a haven for Quakers, allowed religious freedom to anyone following a monotheistic (one God) religion.

(8) The capital of Pennsylvania was name Philadelphia, meaning "Brotherly love." It is a port city and had grown to become the largest city in colonial America by 1750.

(9) Many religious dissenters from Germany migrated to Pennsylvania and were welcomed by Penn.

Quotes from William Penn

The jealous are troublesome to others, but a torment to themselves.

A true friend freely, advises justly, assists readily, adventures boldly, takes all patiently, defends courageously, and continues a friend unchangeably.

Justice is the insurance which we have on our lives and property. Obedience is the premium which we pay for it.

Right is right, even if everyone is against it, and wrong is wrong, even if everyone is for it.

Knowledge is the treasure of a wise man.

Truth often suffers more by the heat of its defenders than the arguments of its opposers.

A good End cannot sanctify evil Means; nor must we ever do Evil, that Good may come of it.

Force may make hypocrites, but it can never make converts.

James Oglethorpe (1696-1785) and Georgia

(1) As a member of the British Parliament, James Oglethorpe investigated prisons in England and was deeply concerned with the plight of those assigned to "debtors' prisons."

(2) Oglethorpe proposed the colonization of what became known as Georgia as a refuge for impoverished people. Colonist were recruited from the streets of the large cities and from debtors' prisons.

(3) The King of England was convinced of the plan to colonize Georgia because this colony would stop Spanish colonial encroachment from Florida.

(4) At Oglethorpe's insistence, slavery and alcohol were initially prohibited in Georgia.

(5) Oglethorpe negotiated the purchase of that land with indigenous leaders and maintain good relations with the indigenous tribes in Georgia, respecting their rights and their cultures.

(6) The colony of Georgia did not have good relations with its neighbor, South Carolina, during the time of Oglethorpe's rule, because escaped slaves could find sanctuary in Georgia.

(7) Oglethorpe permitted members of persecuted religions, including Jews (non-Christians) to settle in Georgia. Rhode Island and Pennsylvania were the only other two colonies which were so enlightened at the time.

(8) James Oglethorpe commanded the Georgia militia in a war with Spanish Florida and received the support of the Creek nation as an ally.

(9) Oglethorpe was prohibited by the charter of Georgia from receiving any money from the colony for his work (which was considerable).

(10) Oglethorpe left Georgia in 1743. Soon after that the ban of slavery was lifted.

(11) Cotton seeds had been brought to Georgia with the first colonists. Cotton growing would become the leading industry of Georgia. Georgia would become the leading cotton growing state in the nineteenth century. Sadly, because cotton growing

created a strong demand for labor, Georgia would also become a leading importer of slaves.

Quotes from James Oglethorpe

If we allow slaves, we act against the very principles by which we associated together, which was to relieve the distressed.

In America there are fertile lands sufficient to support all the useless poor in England, and distressed Protestants in Europe; yet thousands starve for want of sustenance.

Benjamin Franklin (1706-1790), American Genius

In Colonial Times

(1) Benjamin Franklin was born in Boston. He had 16 siblings.

(2) Franklin attended school only to the age of 10. Then he worked as an apprentice on his brother's newspaper.

(3) At age 17 Franklin moved to Philadelphia where he was employed as a printer/typesetter in the newspaper business.

(4) From Philadelphia, Franklin went to London and lived there briefly. He worked in the newspaper business and attended the coffeehouses where men discussed books and the issues of the day.

(5) Franklin returned to Philadelphia in 1726 and lived there for the rest of his life, except for some years he spent in Paris as the American emissary to France.

(6) In 1727 in Philadelphia, Franklin organized at group of men into a discussion, "Junto" club, modeled on the London coffeehouse culture.

(7) Franklin established a publishing business in Philadelphia, publishing a newspaper, *The Pennsylvania Gazette*, and his popular *Poor Richard's Almanack*.

(8) Franklin established the first public library in Philadelphia.

(9) Franklin established the Philadelphia Fire Department.

(10) Benjamin Franklin conducted experiments with electricity, including his famous experiment with a key on a kite string in an electrical storm. He engaged the scientific community regarding his findings, and gained a reputation as a leading scientist.

(11) Franklin founded the University of Pennsylvania.

(12) Franklin organized the American Philosophical Society and served as its first secretary and later as its president.

(13) Franklin established the first colonial postal service.

(14) As the French and Indian War was beginning, Franklin called a meeting of leaders from all the colonies (the Albany Congress) and the Iroquois of New York to plan collective action against the French. Seven colonies sent representatives. This was the first ever meeting of top colonial leaders from various colonies.

During the American Revolution

(15) Franklin served along with Thomas Jefferson and John Adams on the central committee charged with writing the Declaration of Independence.

(16) Franklin served along with Thomas Jefferson as a representative of the colonies to France during the American Revolution. During his stay in Paris, Franklin was a major celebrity.

(17) Benjamin Franklin's son, William, remained loyal to the British cause during the Revolutionary War and continued to serve as Royal Governor of New Jersey until 1776.

After the American Revolution

(18) Franklin, at the age of 81, was a highly esteemed delegate to the Constitutional Convention in 1787.

(19) Benjamin Franklin's image is on the one hundred dollar bill.

Quotes from Benjamin Franklin

A stitch in time saves nine.

A penny saved is a penny earned.

Time is money.

Keep both eyes wide open before marriage; one half closed after.

God heals, but the doctor takes the fee.

Nothing is certain but death and taxes.

An investment in knowledge pays the best interest.

Tell me and I forget. Teach me and I remember. Involve me and I learn.

By failing to prepare, you are preparing to fail.

Well done is better than well said.

It takes many good deeds to build a good reputation, and only one bad one to lose it.

The Constitution only gives people the right to pursue happiness. You have to catch it yourself.

Energy and persistence conquer all things.

Honesty is the best policy.

Any fool can criticize, condemn and complain – and most fools do.

Tricks and treachery are the practice of fools, that don't have brains enough to be honest.

Diligence is the mother of good luck.

Lost time is never found again.

He that is good for making excuses is seldom good for anything else.

Whatever is begun in anger ends in shame.

Write your injuries in dust, your benefits in marble.

Speak ill of no man, but speak all the good you know of everybody.

CHAPTER 2

AMERICAN IDENTITY AND AMERICAN REVOLUTION, 1763-1783

By 1754 English colonist were moving west, expanding into the Ohio Valley while French colonists were moving south into the same region. The French had indigenous allies among the Algonquian people of Canada and the Great Lakes region. The English had indigenous allies, among the nations of the Iroquois Confederation. War began when a small band of Virginia militia under young George Washington fired on a small party of French and their allies in the Ohio Valley.[7] This conflict grew into the French and Indian War in America and the Seven Years War worldwide.

English victory in 1763 set England's American colonies on the path toward revolution. The French had been swept from North America. With no foreign threat on their northern border, the colonists felt no need for the protection of the British army. At the same time, the English Parliament was coping with a huge debt incurred by fighting a long war in defense of their American colonies. Parliament reasonably expected that the colonies would pay some portion of the cost of the war. The American colonists would have to pay taxes. The colonists had never before been required to pay. American colonists claimed that they could not be taxed because they were not represented in Parliament. A strong

---

[7] Soon after this Washington surrendered the fort he had constructed and was released upon signing surrender documents (written in French) in which he accepted responsibility for starting hostilities.

anti-tax movement confronted an equally stubborn Parliament in an ever expanding quarrel.

More British soldiers were sent to America to enforce the tax policies. This in turn created more resentment in the colonies. A pivotal event occurred in Boston in March 1770. Colonists were harassing a squad of British soldiers, throwing snowballs and rocks. The soldiers panicked and fired into the crowd, killing five. Boston newspapers propagandized the event, calling it the "Boston Massacre." Hostilities in Boston continued. Three years later (1773) Boston's "Sons of Liberty" staged the Boston Tea Party to protest a tea tax recently imposed by Parliament. More than 300 chests of tea from three ships were dumped into Boston Harbor. Parliament responded by issuing a series of laws to punish Boston. Bostonians labeled these laws the "Intolerable Acts" (1774). More British soldiers were brought to Boston to enforce the laws, and hostilities between British soldiers and Boston colonists accelerated. In April 1775 the shooting war began at Lexington, Massachusetts, 14 miles inland from Boston.

John Adams (1735-1826) and Boston

During the American Revolution

(1) John Adams of Boston was among the first colonial leaders to openly advocate for independence.

(2) John was the cousin of Samuel Adams, who was also a revolutionary leader opposed to British taxes.

(3) Like other Bostonians, John Adams resented the presence of British troops in the city. Despite his feelings, Adams agreed to represent the soldiers involved in the Boston Massacre. He provided a vigorous defense, and all of the soldiers were acquitted.

(4) John Adams served, along with Thomas Jefferson and Benjamin Franklin, on the central committee to draft the Declaration of Independence.

(5)   During the Revolutionary War, Adams served briefly as ambassador to France, then as ambassador to the Netherlands.

After the establishment of the US Constitution

(6)   John Adams served as vice-president under George Washington (1789-1797).

(7)   John Adams was the second President of the United States (1797-1801).

(8)   During his presidency, John Adams came into conflict with his vice-president, Thomas Jefferson. The two came to lead two opposing political parties and became bitter enemies for many years.

(9)   President Adams built up the US Navy. He is called "the Father of the Navy."

(10) Wars between France and the other European countries broke out after the French Revolution of 1789. Adams fought an undeclared naval war with France during his presidency, as the government of the French Revolution attempted to sever trade between the US and England.

(11) The Federalist Party of President Adams pushed two unpopular, undemocratic laws through Congress limiting free speech in reaction to domestic pressure to side with Revolutionary France in its wars with England (Alien Act and Sedition Act). This heightened the party rivalry and the rift between Adams and Jefferson.

(12) President Adams lost his bid for reelection to Thomas Jefferson in 1800.

(13) In the election of 1800, the Democratic-Republican Party of Thomas Jefferson won a lopsided victory. They would have large majorities in both house of Congress, and the Presidency. To counter the rising power of the opposing party, the outgoing Federalist controlled Congress created a large number of new federal judges, thereby, insuring Federalist control of the judicial branch of government for years to come. In the last days and hours of his Presidency, John Adams was signing appointments

of federal judges, who would be called "the midnight judges" because the legend is that Adams was making these appointments right up to midnight of his last day as President.

(14) Toward the end of their lives Adams and Jefferson exchanged a series of letters by which they mended their long-time feud. Jefferson died early on July 4, 1826. Adams was dying on the same day. Adams' last words were reported to have been, "Mr. Jefferson still lives?" Adams actually died a few hour after Jefferson. This was the fiftieth anniversary of the signing of the Declaration of Independence.

(15) John Adams was the father of John Quincy Adams and the grandfather of Henry Adams. John Quincy Adams also became President, and Henry Adams became a great American historian.

Quotes from John Adams

I must study politics and war that my sons may have liberty to study mathematics and philosophy.

Liberty cannot be preserved without general knowledge among the people.

The happiness of society is the end of government.

Facts are stubborn things; and whatever may be our wishes, our inclinations, or the dictates of our passions, they cannot alter the state of facts and evidence.

Because power corrupts, society's demands for moral authority and character increase as the importance of the position increases.

Great is the guilt of an unnecessary war.

Let us tenderly and kindly cherish, therefore, the means of knowledge. Let us dare to read, think, speak, and write.

A government of laws, and not of men.

Thomas Jefferson (1743-1826) and the Declaration of Independence

How One Sentence Created a Nation

During the American Revolution

(1) Thomas Jefferson wrote *one sentence* which set the course of the American Nation.

(2) Thomas Jefferson was born to a wealthy Virginia family.

(3) Jefferson played the violin for his own amusement.

(4) Jefferson could read several languages.

(5) Jefferson was the architect of his own mansion, Monticello. Monticello is an official National Landmark today.

(6) Jefferson professed to be a Deist. Deism was a popular religious movement during the Enlightenment. Deists believe in a Creator, who is uninvolved in the operations of his creation. When questioned about Christianity, Jefferson said that he was more Christian than most people because he believed in following the example and moral teachings of Christ.

(7) Jefferson was a man of many accomplishments, but he is most known as the author of the Declaration of Independence, the second sentence of which has become the American creed to which we continue to strive today. Jefferson wrote,

> *"We hold these truths to be self-evident, that all men are created equal, that they are endowed by their creator with certain unalienable rights, that among these are life, liberty, and the pursuit of happiness."*

The idea of "equality" for all men (now all people) was not taken seriously until well into the twentieth century. At the time that Jefferson wrote this sentence, he had to be very careful. Most of the 13 colonies waging the war had slavery, and the southern colonies depended on slave labor. Jefferson personally owned hundreds of slaves. A bolder statement about equality, or any statement about slavery, would have been unacceptable to the

Continental Congress. But this one sentence of the Declaration is now universally accepted at face value. Equality under the law is seen as a vital component of liberty and a core value of the United States. If Jefferson had done nothing else, that one sentence would still make him one of the most influential people in history.

Jefferson is considered by many to have been a genius. Could he have been planting a seed in 1776 which he expected to sprout later? Five years after the Declaration, Jefferson wrote, "I tremble for my country when I reflect that God is just; that his justice cannot sleep forever."[8]

(8)   Though a slave owner himself, Jefferson actually introduced a bill in the Continental Congress to prohibit slavery in all the states. It had little support and was quickly voted down. Years earlier he had introduced a bill in the Virginian House of Burgesses to emancipate all the slaves. This was also quickly rejected.

After the American Revolution

(9)   Jefferson served as Minister to France during and after the Revolutionary War. He did not participate in the Constitutional Convention of 1787 because he was in France at the time.

(10) Asked to comment on the Constitution as it was first published, Jefferson gave his tentative approval with the comment that it lacked a bill of rights. The process of debate and ratification was in full swing at the time. To try to make any constitutional changes now, before ratification, would be impossible. Backers of the Constitution proposed that it be passed as is. Then when Congress of the new government met, it could adopt a bill of rights. That pledge was fulfilled. The first US Congress passed ten amendments to the Constitution. These ten amendments are known as "the Bill of Rights."

(11) As Jefferson's wife was dying in 1782, he promised her that he would never remarry, and he didn't. But he is alleged to have had

---

[8] Jefferson, Thomas, Notes on the State of Virginia, Chapter 18, 1781.

a long-time sexual relationship with a slave, Sally Hemmings. DNA evidence today tends to confirm the claim, and all of Ms. Hemming's children were granted their freedom in Jefferson's will.

(12) Jefferson served as Secretary of State under George Washington. During that service he came into conflict with Treasury Secretary Alexander Hamilton over the power of the Federal government. Hamilton wanted to create a Bank of the United States to help regulate and grow the economy. Jefferson, fearing dictatorial power, wanted a Federal government strictly confined by the Constitution, and nothing in the Constitution provided for anything like a federally operated bank.

(13) Jefferson was elected Vice-president in 1796 under President John Adams. Adams, like Hamilton, clashed with Jefferson over the power of the Federal government. The main result of these conflicts was the development of two opposing political parties—the Federalist Party of Hamilton and Adams, and the Democratic-Republican Party of Jefferson.

(14) While he was Vice-president, Jefferson was elected President of the American Philosophical Society.

(15) While Jefferson was Vice-president, he anonymously authored the Virginia Resolution which assert the right of a state, Virginia, to nullify an unconstitutional federal law, the Sedition Act. The Supreme Court had not yet established the principle of "judicial review."[9]

(16) As originally designed in the Constitution, the members of the Electoral College each had two votes with no distinction between President and Vice-president. The candidate who received a majority of Electoral votes would become President, the second place finisher would be Vice-president. This system had created the awkward condition with Federalist President John Adams and Vice-President Thomas Jefferson of the opposing party. In the 1801 election, the Federalist Party was basically discredited by the undemocratic Alien and Sedition Acts. The Democratic-Republicans were poised to take power. The plan was for

---

[9] By Judicial review the Supreme Court may declare a law unconstitutional. This tradition was begun with the case of *Marbury vs. Madison* in 1803.

Jefferson to be President with Aaron Burr as Vice-President. The election result was that Jefferson and Burr were essentially tied. In accordance with the Constitution, the selection of the President was deferred to the House of Representatives. Given the choice between Jefferson and Burr, Alexander Hamilton, leader of the Federalist, distrusting Burr, threw his support to Jefferson. This was the beginning of the feud between Hamilton and Burr which eventually resulted in the duel in which Burr killed Hamilton.

The other result of this election is that Congress became aware that the presidential election process needed changing. The Twelfth Amendment was passed whereby the members of the Electoral College still each had two votes, but the votes would be designated one for President and one for Vice-President.

(17) President Jefferson purchased the Louisiana Territory, the huge section of land between the Mississippi River and the Rocky Mountains, from Napoleonic France in 1803, doubling the size of the US instantly. He then sent the explorers, Meriwether Lewis and William Clark, to map and report about this new land.

(18) Like Presidents Washington and Adams before him, Jefferson continued to have problems with England and France interfering with American trade as these two countries continued to fight each other. He addressed the problem by severely restricting American trade. This policy greatly damaged the American economy (especially in the North) while having little effect on the warring countries. As a result, Jefferson's popularity was greatly diminished during his last years in office, and the problem of trade interference continued.

(19) President Jefferson served two full terms before stepping down, reaffirming the tradition established by George Washington of no third term.

(20) Jefferson founded the University of Virginia and did all the surveying work to plan the campus himself.

(21) Jefferson amassed a large personal library which he sold to the US so that a Library of Congress could be reestablished after the British had destroyed the books in the first Library of Congress during the War of 1812.

(22) Thomas Jefferson and John Adams both died on July 4, 1826, the fiftieth anniversary of the signing of the Declaration of Independence. Jefferson had written the document and Adams had been directly involved in its editing.

(23) Thomas Jefferson's image is on the two dollar bill and the nickel.

Quotes from Thomas Jefferson

Honesty is the first chapter in the book of wisdom.

Nothing can stop the man with the right mental attitude from achieving his goal; nothing on earth can help the man with the wrong mental attitude.

I like the dreams of the future better than the history of the past.

Do you want to know who you are? Don't ask. Act! Action will delineate and define you.

When angry count to ten before you speak. If very angry, count to one hundred.

I never considered a difference of opinion in politics, in religion, in philosophy, as cause for withdrawing from a friend.

Educate and inform the whole mass of the people... They are the only sure reliance for the preservation of our liberty.

He who knows best knows how little he knows.

Where the press is free and every man able to read, all is safe.

George Washington (1732-1799), Father of His Country

The French and Indian War

(1) George Washington's first career was as a surveyor.

(2) Washington led a small party of Virginia militia into the Ohio Valley in 1754. They discovered a French fort, Fort Duquesne. Washington's men then constructed their own fort, Fort Necessity. In a chance encounter with the French, Washington's men fired on them. This began the French and Indian War which spread throughout the British and French empires and became known to the world as the Seven Years War. Washington's fort was captured and he was forced to sign the surrender documents (written in French) by which he accepted responsibility for starting the war. He was then released.

(3) Washington was a Virginia militia commander under British General James Braddock in 1755, when Braddock's forces, advancing into the Ohio Valley, were encountered by a force of Indians supported by the French. Braddock attempted to use standard European military tactics against an opponent which disbursed and took cover behind trees. The battle went badly and Braddock was killed. Washington is credited with helping to avoid a complete disaster by rallying much of the combined British and colonial forces. In the course of the battle, Washington accumulated several bullet holes in his jacket and hat and had two horses shot out from under him, but he was not even scratched. This was the last battle of Washington's military career prior to the American Revolutionary War.

(4) Washington did have false teeth, but they were not wooden.

During the American Revolution

(5) Washington was nominated to lead the Continental Army by John Adams largely because he looked the part and fit the bill. Washington was an imposing figure. He was 6 foot 3 at a time when the average soldier in his army was 5 foot 6; he had military

experience, though it was not extensive nor entirely successful; and, perhaps most importantly, he was from Virginia. Virginia was the largest southern colony. The war had begun in Massachusetts, where anti-British feeling was strongest, and all the early action was there. If the British had been able to confine the war to Massachusetts, the colonists would have had little prospect for success.

(6)   After receiving his commission, Washington went immediately to Massachusetts to take charge of the war as commander of the Continental Army. No Continental Army yet existed, but Washington was expected to form one around the Massachusetts militia.

(7)   Washington's first action was a success. He was able to have artillery brought from the captured Fort Ticonderoga in New York to Dorchester Heights in Boston. Under cover of darkness, Washington's men placed the guns on the Heights overlooking Boston Harbor. The next day, the British forces in Boston found that they were in grave danger from the guns. The British army in Boston boarded British ships in the harbor and left. If Washington's forces had fired on the ships, they would likely have inflicted heavy damage. But this was 1775, early in the war, Washington may have felt that reconciliation with England was still possible.

(8)   Washington had few victories in the Revolution. He was faced with a superior military force in terms numbers, equipment, and training. He soon learned the futility of confronting the British directly when his army was nearly captured in New York City. His genius and contribution were in that he was able to keep the army together, strike the enemy, and run away.

(9)   Washington had a major victory when his army crossed the Delaware River on Christmas night 1776 to attack the enemy in Trenton, New Jersey. He was in desperate need of a victory at that time. His army had had no success for a year and the enlistments of many of his soldiers were about to expire. He chose Trenton as a target partly because the British defenses there were manned by German mercenary soldiers hired to fight. American colonists were especially angry that the king had hired foreign soldiers to fight them. The night crossing and early morning attack caught

these Germans by complete surprise. Nine hundred foreign fighters were captured and 22 were killed. Two Americans died and five were wounded. Washington had inspired his men to continue the struggle.

(10) Washington was able to learn as the war continued and became skilled at hit and run tactics.

(11) When the British general, Charles Cornwallis was trapped at Yorktown, Virginia in 1781, the French navy blockaded the harbor and Washington rushed down from the north. Cornwallis surrendered his entire army of 7000 men. This did not really end the American Revolution. The British general, Clinton, still had a several thousand men garrisoned in New York City, and the British still controlled the southern ports of Charleston and Savannah, but the war in the south had now turned around, and American forces were in control of New England. Meanwhile, the attention of the British was directed to more dangerous threats. Spain and the Netherlands joined a coalition with France against the British. The final peace treaty had to wait for the French to conclude their portion of the war. The Treaty of Paris ending all hostilities was signed in 1783.

(12) Washington resisted the encouragement of his military colleagues of the Society of Cincinnati to seize power and declared himself king immediately after the conclusion of the Revolutionary War.

After the American Revolution

(13) The new United States were ruled under the Articles of Confederation, but this weak confederation proved a failure. In 1787 a convention, which met in Philadelphia with George Washington as president, wrote a constitution, forming a federal government.

(14) Washington was elected unanimously to be the first President of the United States with his term starting in 1789. He served two full terms then retired. This began the tradition of no third term for American presidents.

(15) As America's first president, George Washington molded the Executive Department of government. He created the first Cabinet which consisted of the Secretaries of State, Treasury, and War, and the Attorney General of the United States.

(16) George Washington, like most wealthy Virginia landowners of his time, owned slaves and never publicly expressed any opposition to slavery. On the other hand, he did provide in his will that all his slaves would be freed upon the death of his wife, and his wife, Martha, did free all his slaves a year after his death.

(17) George Washington's famous Farewell Address was never delivered orally. It was published in a major Philadelphia newspaper. In it, Washington warned his fellow countrymen to beware of "entangling alliances" and political parties. Europe was in turmoil due to the French Revolution, and a French ambassador, "Citizen" Edmond Genet, had tried to sway American public opinion in favor of France. Washington warned that America was a young and fragile country. If it got dragged into the wars in Europe, the hard won independence of America could be lost. He also felt that political parties would behave like warring factions and destroy the country. Presidents Adams and Jefferson, who succeeded Washington, heeded his warning about entangling alliances but disregarded the advice about political parties.

(18) George Washington's Mount Vernon home on the bank of the Potomac River near Alexandria, Virginia, is a National Historic Landmark.

(19) George Washington's image is on the dollar bill and the quarter.

Quotes from George Washington

It is far better to be alone, than to be in bad company.

Truth will ultimately prevail where there is pains to bring it to light.

Happiness and moral duty are inseparably connected.

It is better to offer no excuse than a bad one.

CHAPTER 3

ESTABLISHING THE EARLY REPUBLIC, 1783-1830

Chronology

1775-1789	Weak association of independent states under The Articles of Confederation
1787	Constitutional Convention
1789-1797	Presidency of George Washington, Father of His Country
1797-1801	Presidency of John Adams, Father of the Navy
1801-1809	Presidency of Thomas Jefferson, Author of the Declaration of Independence
1809-1817	Presidency of James Madison, Father of the Constitution
1817-1825	Presidency of James Monroe, The Monroe Doctrine
1825-1829	Presidency of John Quincy Adams, son of President John Adams
1829-1837	Presidency of Andrew Jackson, Jacksonian Democracy

After the Revolutionary War, the newly independent colonies called themselves the United States, implying that they were 13 independent countries. Their association was a confederation with rules of association called The Article of Confederation. The states struggled economically under The Articles and discovered that they were all too small to function efficiently as independent states. They needed to unite into one nation. In 1787 representatives of all 13 states met in Philadelphia and wrote a constitution for one united country.

The new government was established in 1789 with George Washington as the first President of the United States, the world's first modern democracy. The direction of that democracy was yet to be established—foreign relations, questions of citizenship, who would participate and who would be left out, what this new democracy would become. These issues were often decided in struggle and the direction of the struggle was not always positive.

James Madison (1751-1836), Father of the Constitution

Writing and Ratifying the Constitution

(1) James Madison was a member of the Continental Congress during and after the Revolutionary War.

(2) Madison was a representative of Virginia at the Constitutional Convention. He had researched how other governments had been organized and came to the convention with many good ideas which were adopted into the Constitution.

(3) After the Constitution had been written, individual states had to ratify it. The convention had agreed that when nine states ratified the Constitution it would go into effect, but it was hoped that all the states would ratify and join the Union. In New York and Virginia the Constitution was debated extensively. Those in favor of the Constitution became known as Federalists; those opposed were Anti-federalists. To build support for the Constitution, James Madison, Alexander Hamilton, and John Jay wrote a series of articles in New York newspapers explaining how the new government would work. These articles were later collected into *The Federalist Papers*. *The Federalist Papers* are still studied in universities today because they brilliantly explain the Constitution.

(4) James Madison stood 5 feet 4 inches tall and weighed about 100 pounds.

The New Republic

(5)   James Madison was Secretary of State under President Thomas Jefferson. Because Jefferson was not married, Madison's wife, Dolly, sometimes acted as hostess for White House events during Jefferson's presidency. Since Madison succeeded Jefferson as President, Dolly Madison was the White House hostess for 16 years.

(6)   When James Madison became President in 1809, he inherited the problem of foreign interference with American shipping, as the Napoleonic Wars continued.

(7)   In 1812 by a close vote in Congress, the United States declared war on Great Britain. Interference with American shipping, impressment (hijacking) of American sailors into the British navy, and British encouragement and support for indigenous resistance on the frontier were the causes of the war.

The war was unpopular in New England where trade with Great Britain was important to the economy. New England politicians labeled it "Mr. Madison's War."

(8)   In September 1814 an American lawyer, Francis Scott Key, was detained aboard a British ship as it shelled Fort McHenry near Baltimore. Key watched the battle all night and was pleased to see that the American flag was still flying over the fort the next morning. The attack had been unsuccessful. Key was inspired to write a poem about the battle. It was later set to music and became "The Star Spangled Banner", our National Anthem.

(9)   In 1814 the US government fled Washington, DC, as the British attacked. The British burned the Capitol building and the White House. Dolly Madison remained in the capital until the last minute, directing workers as to which White House treasures were to be loaded on carts for rescue.

(10)   A convention of leaders of the New England States (northeast), unhappy with "Mr. Madison's War", met in Hartford, Connecticut and discussed a proposal that they secede from the Union.

Quotes from James Madison

If men were angels, no government would be necessary.

The happy Union of these States is a wonder; their Constitution a miracle; … example the hope of Liberty throughout the world.

The people are the only legitimate fountain of power, and it is from them that the constitutional charter, under which the several branches of government hold their power, is derived.

The truth is that all men having power ought to be mistrusted.

Knowledge will forever govern ignorance; and a people who mean to be their own governors must arm themselves with the power which knowledge gives.

In Republics, the great danger is, that the majority may not sufficiently respect the rights of the minority.

To the press alone, chequered as it is with abuses, the world is indebted for all the triumphs which have been gained by reason and humanity over error and oppression.

The advancement and diffusion of knowledge is the only guardian of true liberty.

Alexander Hamilton (1757-1804), Father of the National Debt

(1) As Treasury Secretary under President George Washington, Alexander Hamilton insisted that the US honor the Revolutionary War debt of the Continental Congress and assume the foreign debts of all the states in full. This was somewhat unpopular and opposed by Secretary of State Thomas Jefferson. As much of this debt had appeared to be uncollectible, speculators had

bought up large amounts of the debt at ten cents on the dollar. Hamilton's plan would make a few speculators very rich, but would also establish the solid credit of the United States and eliminate the problem of having individual states indebted to foreign governments.

(2) Alexander Hamilton was born out of wedlock in the British West Indies.

(3) Hamilton was an aide to General Washington during the Revolutionary War.

(4) Hamilton was one of three authors of *The Federalist Papers*, articles written for New York newspapers to convince New Yorkers to ratify the Constitution.

(5) President Washington appointed Hamilton as America's first Secretary of the Treasury.

(6) As secretary of the Treasury, Hamilton advocated for the expansion of the power of the Federal government, using the doctrine of "implied powers." This brought him into conflict with Thomas Jefferson, who insisted on strict interpretation of the Constitution. The specific issue involved was Hamilton's proposal that the Congress charter a Bank of the United States. Hamilton felt this would be necessary and proper to put the country on sound financial ground, though the Constitution did not give Congress the authority to do this. Jefferson lost this battle, too.

(7) Political differences between Alexander Hamilton and Thomas Jefferson led to the creation of two opposing political parties. The Federalists, who wanted to expand the power of the central government, were led by Hamilton and John Adams. The Democratic-Republicans, who wanted strict interpretation of the Constitution, were led by Jefferson and James Madison. Merchants and bankers of the northeast tended to be Federalists. Farmers of the south and the west gravitated to the Democratic-Republican Party.

(8) In the 1801 presidential election when no one got a majority of the Electoral College vote and the decision was left to the House of Representatives, the Federalists had no chance because the

vast majority in the House were Democratic-Republicans, but the Federalists had enough votes to decide which Democratic-Republican would win. Hamilton threw his support to Thomas Jefferson, explaining that Jefferson was an honest man who could be trusted; Jefferson's opponent, Aaron Burr was not (according to Hamilton). Jefferson won and became President. Burr became Vice-president.

(9) The animosity between Hamilton and Burr continued until 1804 when Burr shot and killed Hamilton in a dual.

(10) Alexander Hamilton's image is on the ten dollar bill.

Quotes from Alexander Hamilton

There is a certain enthusiasm in liberty that makes human nature rise above itself, in acts of bravery and heroism.

I think the first duty of society is justice.

Unless your government is respectable, foreigners will invade your rights…

In framing a government which is to be administered by men over men, the great difficulty lies in this: you must first enable the government to control the governed; and in the next place, oblige it to control itself.

Real firmness is good for anything; strut is good for nothing.

The nation which can prefer disgrace to danger is prepared for a master and deserves one.

Real liberty is neither found in despotism or the extremes of democracy, but in moderate governments.

Tecumseh (1768-1813) and the Shawnee Confederacy

(1) Tecumseh was a Shawnee chief who hoped to establish an independent indigenous nation in the region of the Ohio Valley with a help of the British in Canada.

(2) Shawnees had battled off-and-on against Anglo-American expansion since the French and Indian War of 1756-1763. Tecumseh's father was killed in battle in 1774. A brother was killed in battle in 1788, and another brother was killed in the famous Battle of Fallen Timbers in 1794.

(3) Tecumseh played a minor role as a scout for the Shawnee-Miami coalition in the defeat of General Arthur St. Clair at the Battle of the Wabash in 1790. St. Clair lost 600 soldiers killed in the worst defeat of American forces by indigenous people ever.

(4) Tecumseh was the political-military leader of his movement. His brother, Tenskwatawa, was the spiritual leader. At its zenith, Tecumseh's confederacy included more than two dozen indigenous nations.

(5) Tecumseh's nemesis was Indiana Governor William Henry Harrison, who would later be elected President of the United States.

(6) In a meeting between the Shawnee and Harrison, Harrison challenged Tenskwatawa's claim to supernatural powers, and Tenskwatawa stated that he would demonstrate his powers by stopping the sun. The Shawnee Prophet predicted the day this would happen. On that day, an eclipse of the sun occurred, and Tenskwatawa's reputation was enhanced.

(7) In 1811 as tension between indigenous people and Anglo-Americans increased and Tecumseh was away from his country trying to recruit tribes in the south to join him, a battle broke out at Tippecanoe Creek. Harrison's men won and Tenskwatawa was disgraced for having told his people that his magic would protect them from the enemy's bullets. This was a major blow to Tecumseh's confederacy from which it never fully recovered. No indigenous alliance as large as Tecumseh had assembled would ever be brought together again in North America.

(8) During the War of 1812 Tecumseh allied his forces with the British, fighting in the Great Lakes region. He defeated American forces in Michigan Territory and captured Fort Detroit, when the American commander surrendered to Tecumseh's numerically inferior force without a fight.

(9) The Shawnee were known to torture prisoners. Tecumseh found this unacceptable and forcefully denounced torture.

(10) Tecumseh was killed in 1813 in the Battle of the Thames.

Quotes by Tecumseh

When you rise in the morning, give thanks for the light, for your life, for your strength. Give thanks for your food and for the joy of living. If you see no reason to give thanks, the fault lies in yourself.

Show respect to all people, but grovel to none.

Let us form one body, one heart, and defend to the last warrior our country, our homes, our liberty, and the graves of our fathers.

When the legends die, the dreams end; there is no more greatness.

A single twig breaks, but the bundle of twigs is strong.

Sequoyah (c. 1770-1843) and the Cherokee Literacy

(1) Sequoyah, a member of the Cherokee nation, was operating a trading post, when inspired by his white store patrons' use of written language, he developed a system for written Cherokee.

(2) Sequoyah was born around 1770 in what is now Tennessee. His father, who was not involved in his life, may have been a white man. Sequoyah's English name was George Gist.

(3) Sequoyah had been permanently crippled in a hunting accident at an early age.

(4) Sequoyah's early career was as a silversmith, blacksmith, and trading post proprietor.

(5) Sequoyah served in a Cherokee regiment of the American army during the Red Stick War against hostile Creeks, which culminated with the 1813 Battle of Horseshoe Bend.

(6) Sequoyah is reported to have become somewhat addicted to alcohol while he was operating his trading post. He overcame his addiction and discontinued selling alcohol at his store.

(7) The Cherokee Nation adopted Sequoyah's writing system in 1825.

(8) In 1828 the Cherokee Nation began publication of the *Cherokee Phoenix*, the first newspaper to be published in an indigenous American language.

(9) Sequoyah's writing system was popular among the Cherokee, and soon the literacy rate among the Cherokee exceeded that of their Anglo-American neighbors.

(10) Sequoyah promoted his writing system to other tribes, and news of its success spread widely. His system became a model for many others, in North America from Georgia to Alaska, in Africa among the transplanted former slaves of Liberia, and as far away as China.

(11) In 1828 Sequoya visited Washington, DC, as part of a Cherokee delegation to negotiate a treaty for a Cherokee reservation in Indian Territory (Oklahoma). While there, he sat for the famous portrait of him with pipe in mouth and his script in hand.

(12) Sequoya visited indigenous tribes in New Mexico Territory to spread his ideas of written language while that region was still under Spanish control.

(13) Sequoya saw some advantage in Indian Territory that most other Cherokee did not see. He was among the first of his people to migrate there voluntarily in 1829.

CHAPTER 4

EXPANSION, AND EXCLUSION, 1828-1848

In 1828 America's greatest hero of the War of 1812, General Andrew Jackson, was elected President, beginning what was to be known as "the Age of Jackson," marked by expansion of Democracy among white men. Women and non-whites were, however, excluded. Indigenous people, some of whom hoped for a degree in inclusion, were rejected, as Jackson supported a plan to force all indigenous people east of the Mississippi River to relocate to Indian Territory (Oklahoma).

Jackson was a popular President and generally remains a popular figure in American history, but he, like America, had a dark side undeserving of emulation.[10]

By 1848 the American Nation would extend from ocean to ocean, but the process of expansion is not glorious. Anglo-American settlers had been invited into Texas in 1824. Twelve years later Sam Houston, the former Governor of Tennessee, led a revolution and overthrew the rule of Mexico in Texas. The United States annexed Texas in 1844. Then in 1846 President James K. Polk appears to have provoked a war with Mexico which resulted in the annexation of California and New Mexico Territory (now the states of New Mexico, Arizona, Nevada, and Utah, and parts of other states).

---

[10] Emulation: the attempt to imitate or exceed due to admiration.

Andrew Jackson (1767-1845) and Jacksonian Democracy

(1) Andrew Jackson's father was killed in a lumbering accident when Andrew was only a baby.

(2) As a boy assisting the American side in the Revolutionary War, Jackson was taken prisoner. When young Andrew refused to shine the boots of a British officer, the officer slashed him with his sword, leaving Jackson scarred for life and deeply resentful of the British.

(3) As captives of the British, Andrew Jackson and his brother contracted smallpox and his brother died from the disease.

(4) Andrew's mother died of cholera which she contracted while serving as a nurse during the Revolutionary War.

(5) Jackson was largely self-educated. He trained himself to be a lawyer.

(6) Andrew Jackson served as Attorney General for the Tennessee Territory. After Tennessee became a state, he was elected to the US House of Representatives, then to the Senate, then to the State Supreme Court.

(7) In 1802 Jackson won election as major general commanding the Tennessee militia.

(8) In 1790 Andrew Jackson had met and fallen in love with Rachel Donelson Robards, a woman who had been in an unhappy marriage with an abusive husband. Rachel had been separated from her husband, who was believed to have secured a divorce. When Jackson married Rachel, it came out that the divorce may not have been finalized. After clearing the legal matter of the divorce, Andrew and Rachel again married in 1794. Scandal plagued the Jacksons and Andrew's political career, as accusations persisted. Andrew Jackson was sensitive to the criticism and quick to defend the honor of Rachel. He fought two duels as a result. In his first duel, Jackson took a bullet in the chest that lodged near his heart and could not be removed. Jackson's opponent stood motionless after taking his shot in accordance with the dueling custom. Jackson then shot and

killed him. Because Jackson had chosen to kill a defenseless man when he could have fired into the air, his reputation was damaged and his career in Tennessee politics was cut short. He carried the bullet in his chest for the rest of his life.

(9)   Much of Jackson's wealth came as a slave owning planter. He owned more than 100 slaves at the time of his death, and he never expressed any criticism of the plantation system. His estate, the Heritage, outside Nashville, Tennessee, is a National Historic Site.

(10) In 1813 Andrew Jackson led Tennessee volunteers and their indigenous allies in defeating the Red Stick Creeks in the Battle of Horseshoe Bend. The Red Stick Creeks had massacred 250 Anglo-Americans at Fort Sims in Alabama. Young Sam Houston, age 21, served under Jackson during this campaign.

(11) In the last major battle of the War of 1812, General Jackson's forces, defending New Orleans, defeated a much larger British army, killing or wounding over 1500 British soldiers with only light losses on the American side. The battle was fought in early January and the war was technically over. A treaty had been signed on Christmas day 1814. The word that peace had been achieved reached the US shortly after Jackson's victory, so many people credited Jackson for saving America, and Jackson became America's greatest war hero at that time. It is possible that if the British had captured New Orleans, they might have been reluctant to surrender it later.

(12) General Jackson led US forces into Florida in 1816 and 1818 in reaction to raids by Seminole Indians and escaped slaves in Georgia. These resulted in the sale of Florida by Spain to the United States. In the 1818 campaign, Jackson was criticized for exceeding his orders and summarily executing two British citizens as spies.[11]

(13) Jackson got a reputation as being "tough as hickory" during his military career, and became affectionately known as "Old Hickory."

---

[11] Summarily: without due process of law.

(14) War hero Andrew Jackson ran for President of the United States in 1824. His vote count in terms of both popular vote and Electoral College vote far exceeded that of any of his three opponents in this four man race, but with the electoral vote split among three of the candidates, Jackson did not have the majority (50%). The election was thrown into the House of Representatives.[12] Henry Clay, who was speaker of the House and one of the four candidates, dropped out of the race declaring his support for John Quincy Adams. This resulted in Adams' election.

When Adams became President, he appointed Clay as Secretary of State. This caused Jackson's supporters to accuse the President and Secretary Clay of a "corrupt bargain." Adams had been Secretary of State, and the three Presidents who had immediately preceded him had all been Secretary of State before becoming President.[13]

(15) Andrew Jackson ran for the Presidency again in 1828. In the course of the campaign, his wife's alleged bigamy was used as an anti-Jackson tactic. Rachel was greatly distressed and died a month after the election. Jackson blamed her death on the criticism she had faced during the campaign.

(16) John Quincy Adams, the son of John Adams, like his father, served only one term as president. In the 1828 election, with the shadow of the "corrupt bargain" hanging over him, he lost a landslide election to Andrew Jackson.

(17) Andrew Jackson, America's seventh President, was its first President from the west (west of the Appalachian Mountains). Thousands of western frontiersmen attended his inauguration. Many got into the White House and damaged furniture with muddy boots. Eastern newspaper reported that the western mob had taken over.

---

[12] This had happened before in the 1800 election between Jefferson and Burr.

[13] John Quincy Adams, James Monroe, James Madison, and Thomas Jefferson had all been Secretary of State, and all but Jefferson had gone immediately from Secretary of State to President.

(18) Upon assuming the Presidency, Andrew Jackson proceeded to replace a large number of officials, even minor officials like local postmasters, with those who had supported his campaign. No previous President had done this, but many after Jackson would follow his example. This policy is commonly known as "the spoils system" from the military adage "to the victors belong the spoils."

(19) Congress had passed a high tariff in 1828 which enraged southerners. In 1832 Congress lowered the tariff somewhat, but southerners were still unhappy. When South Carolina, led by Jackson's vice-president, John C. Calhoun, claimed the right to nullify the law and threatened secession over the tariff issue, Jackson sent a Navy warship to Charleston harbor and threatened to hang any man who worked to support nullification or secession.

The falling out with Calhoun and the threat of secession were highlighted by a famous toast made at a formal dinner. Jackson stood and said in a direct challenge to Calhoun, "To the Union. It must be preserved." Calhoun stood and replied, "To the Union, next to liberty most dear."

(20) Andrew Jackson hated the Bank of the United States and thought that it was unconstitutional. Congressman Henry Clay, planning to run for President against Jackson in 1832, wanted to create a campaign issue. To do this he proposed to re-charter the Bank of the United States that year, though the charter was not yet due to expire. Jackson vetoed the charter, as Clay had expected he would. Clay had his issue, but Jackson won reelection.

At that time Jackson determined to kill the bank himself. He did this by taking federal government funds out of the Bank of the United States and depositing these funds in state "pet banks." The BUS was crippled and a few years later its charter was allowed to expire.

(21) Backers of Andrew Jackson dropped their classification as Democratic-Republicans and began to refer to themselves simply as "Democrats."

(22) During the 1832 campaign, some anti-Jackson cartoons had him riding a donkey. Jackson's Democratic Party embraced the symbol. The donkey has been the symbol of the Democratic Party ever since.

(23) Andrew Jackson was known as "the veto President" though he vetoed only seven major bills. This was more than all six of his predecessors combined. Previous Presidents had reserved the veto only for those bills which appeared to violate the Constitution. Jackson used the veto for any bill with which he disagreed.

(24) Andrew Jackson asserted so much power as President that his opponents began to call him "King Andrew" and a political party formed to oppose him. The new party named themselves the "Whig Party" after the party in England of the same name which opposed the king there.

(25) During the time of Jackson, the franchise (right to vote) was extended in most states by removal of the property ownership requirement. The number of eligible voters (all white men) doubled.

(26) Andrew Jackson backed the Indian Removal Act passed by Congress in 1830, a scheme to illegally usurp[14] land granted in treaties and move all the tribes which were east of the Mississippi River to Indian Territory (present day Oklahoma). He ordered the army to forcefully escort the Indians to their new reservations. This forced march is known as "the Trail of Tears." Among the Cherokee alone up to 6000 people died in detention centers awaiting the march or on the march itself.

(27) Jackson rationalized moving the Indians to Indian Territory (Oklahoma) because there they could live in peace with no threat of Anglo-American encroachment. He predicted that white civilization would not reach that far west for a hundred

---

[14] Usurp: To seize by force.

generations. White civilization actually began encroaching on this land in less than three generations.

(28) The Cherokee sued for the right to the land granted them by treaty and won the decision in the Supreme Court, to which Jackson famously said, "Mr. Marshall (Chief Justice John Marshall) has made his decision. Now let him enforce it."

(29) The forced Indian removal caused at least two significant Indian Wars—the Black Hawk War in Illinois and the Second Seminole War in Florida. The issue for the Seminoles was complicated because they were being asked to turn over the escaped slaves, who were numerous among the Seminoles. This Seminole War was long and costly. It lasted seven years and cost the lives of 1500 US soldiers, most from disease.

(30) When Andrew Jackson left office he had established a record as the oldest American President ever, a record that stood for almost 150 years, final broken by Ronald Reagan.

(31) Andrew Jackson's image is on the twenty dollar bill.

Quotes by Andrew Jackson

Take time to deliberate; but when the time for action arrives, stop thinking and go in.

You must pay the price if you wish to secure the blessing.

Juan Seguin (1806-1890) and Texas Independence

(1) Juan Seguin was born and raised in Texas. His family were prominent leaders in Texas in 1825, the year that Stephen F. Austin was allowed to lead 300 Anglo-American families into Texas.

(2) Seguin was critical of the government of Mexico and a proponent of greater autonomy for Texas.

(3) Seguin was elected mayor of San Antonio for the first time in 1833.

(4)   Seguin sided with Sam Houston's revolutionaries in the Texas revolution and was commissioned a captain.

(5)   Seguin was at the Alamo and escaped death because he was sent to try to get reinforcements.

(6)   As an officer in the Army of Texas, Juan Seguin participated in delaying actions which helped allow Sam Houston time to prepare for the decisive Battle of San Jacinto in which Seguin also participated. Seguin was commended by Houston for his service and promoted to lieutenant colonel.

(7)   After the Texas Revolution, Seguin served in the Texas Senate from 1837 to 1840. He was the only Tejano in the Senate at that time.[15]

(8)   Seguin had interests on both sides of the border. In 1840 he raised a force of Tejanos in support of an associate attempting to stage a rebellion to create a Republic of the Rio Grande. Before Seguin's men had crossed the Nueces River, the rebellion had failed, and Seguin was left to absorb the costs he had incurred.

(9)   In 1841 Seguin was back in Mexico briefly on a self-confessed unsuccessful "smuggling" enterprise. While there, he attained information about an impending invasion which he reported and the information aided Texas defenses.

(10) Seguin was again elected mayor of San Antonio in 1841. At that time he came into conflict with Anglo-American "squatters" who were confiscating Tejano land. He was the last Hispanic mayor of that city for more than a century.

(11) Pre-armed with knowledge of an impending invasion of San Antonio, Seguin alerted the citizens, advising them to abandon the city. Most of the Tejanos took Seguin's advice, but most of the Anglos prepared defenses. Seguin and his family also abandoned the city. When the invasion occurred, many of the Anglo population accused the Tejanos, and Seguin, of complicity. By Seguin's own account, some of the Tejanos may have provided some aid to the Mexican forces.

---

[15] The term "Tejano" refers to someone of Spanish decent who ancestors were living in Texas before Anglo-Americans were allowed to legally come into Texas in 1824.

(12) Seguin joined in the pursuit of the Mexican army after they had withdrawn from San Antonio.

(13) After the 1841 invasion, racial tension in Texas increased. Seguin and his family experience growing harassment. Seguin's authority as mayor was undercut, and an angry mob, which had to be turned away at gun point, appeared at his house. He resigned as mayor and fled with his family to Mexico. He was arrested and chose service in the Mexican Army under Santa Anna to prison. To prove his loyalty to Mexico, Seguin was required to participate in a small raid on Texas. His participation was minimal.

(14) During the Mexican War (1846-1848), Seguin served as an officer in the Mexican Army.

(15) After the Mexican War, Seguin was allowed to return to Texas and was never charged with any serious crime.

(16) Seguin served two terms, four years, as Bexar County Justice of the Peace beginning in 1853.

(17) Seguin published his memoirs in 1858 in answer to his critics in Texas.

(18) Seguin became a Texas Democratic Party organizer in the 1850s.

(19) Juan Seguin returned to Mexico about 1883 and lived there for the last seven years of his life.

Quotes from Juan Seguin

Many a noble heart grasped the sword in defense of the liberty of Texas, cheerfully pouring out their blood for our cause, and to them everlasting public gratitude is due.

I address myself to the American people; to that people impetuous, as the whirlwind, when aroused by the hypocritical clamors of designing men, but just, impartial and composed, whenever men and facts are submitted to their judgment.

Zachary Taylor (1784-1850) and American Blood on American Soil

(1) General Zachary Taylor became famous for his service in the Mexican War of 1846-1848.

(2) Zachary Taylor's father was Richard Taylor, a Virginia plantation owner and former lieutenant colonel in the Revolutionary army. The family moved to Kentucky, near Louisville, when Zachary was young and he grew up on the family plantation there.

(3) Taylor began his military career as a second lieutenant in 1808.

(4) While in the army, Taylor, a wealthy man, purchased a large plantation near Louisville, which included numerous slaves.

(5) In 1811 Captain Taylor took command of Fort Knox, which was under Indian threat, after the previous commander had fled.

(6) In 1812 Taylor commanded Fort Harrison in Indiana Territory and repulsed an attack by Tecumseh. Taylor was subsequently promoted to major.

(7) Zachary Taylor served as a colonel in the Black Hawk War in 1832.

(8) In 1837 during the Second Seminole War, Taylor defeated a large Seminole force in the Battle of Lake Okeechobee, earning a promotion to brigadier general. He was soon placed in charge of the entire US army in Florida and remained in that post, fighting the Seminoles, for two years.

(9) While commanding in the Second Seminole War, General Taylor acquired the nickname "Old Rough and Ready."

(10) In 1844 the US annexed Texas, the breakaway Lone Star Republic, which the Mexicans still claimed. General Taylor was ordered to Louisiana in preparation for a possible war.

(11) Though Mexico had not recognized the independence of Texas and certainly did not recognize the annexation of Texas by the United States, Mexico did unofficially acquiesce to a border between Texas and Mexico at the Nueces River. This is also the border that most Texans recognized. The land between the Nueces and the Rio Grande was contested.

America's new expansionist President, James K. Polk, had made efforts to purchase California from Mexico. The Mexican government had no interest in the proposal. But California might be seized in a war with Mexico. Polk ordered Taylor to lead his command across the Nueces to the Rio Grande, a move which would surely provoke a military reaction by Mexico. The Mexicans did attack and Polk asked Congress for a declaration of war because, the President said, "American blood has been shed on American soil." Congress agreed and declared war.

(12) After the US declared war on Mexico, General Taylor was ordered into Northern Mexico and placed in charge of military operations there. He performed brilliantly, winning several major battles. He was promoted to major general and received Congressional commendations. At the Battle of Buena Vista, General Taylor defeated a much larger Mexican force under Mexican dictator, Antonio Lopez de Santa Anna. This battle cemented Taylor's fame as a war hero.

(13) In 1848 Zachary Taylor accepted the nomination of the Whig Party for President of the United States, though he had no previous party affiliation and, in fact, admitted that he had never, up to that time, actually voted in any election. He won the election, becoming the second Whig Party war hero nominee to be elected President of the United States.[16]

(14) President Taylor, though a southern plantation owner with many slaves, opposed the talk of secession by southern leaders in 1850.

(15) As the country was become dangerously divided over the issue of slavery in 1850, Henry Clay, "the Great Compromiser," proposed the third great north-south compromise of his career, which would give southerners the stringent Fugitive Slave Law they wanted. President Taylor opposed the compromise and

---

[16] William Henry Harrison, the hero of the Battle of Tippecanoe against the Shawnee confederacy, was nominated by the Whig Party and elected in 1840. He refused to wear an overcoat for his inauguration and gave the longest inaugural speech ever up to that time on a very cold day. As a result, he caught pneumonia and died a month later.

threatened to veto it. As debate was going on in Congress, the previously healthy, vigorous President Taylor was suddenly stricken with food poisoning and died. Historians today find this to be suspicious, but it seems to have raise little suspicion at the time. The Compromise of 1850 passed Congress; the new President, Millard Fillmore, signed it; and the secessionist crisis passed for the time being.

Quoted from Zachary Taylor

Never judge a stranger by his clothes.

As to the Constitution and the Union, I have taken an oath to support the one, and I cannot do so without preserving the other …

It would be judicious to act with magnanimity towards a prostrate foe.[17]

Winfield Scott (1786-1866) and the Mexican War

(1) Winfield Scott began a long, distinguished military career in the Virginia militia, commissioned a captain in 1808.

(2) In 1810, Scott was court-martialed for "un-officer-like conduct" due to his criticism of a superior officer and having failed to keep accurate financial records. He was suspended from the army temporarily as punishment.

(3) Winfield Scott was back in the army when the War of 1812 began. He was promoted to lieutenant colonel, but was soon captured by the British. He regained his freedom as a result of a prisoner exchange and went on to serve with distinction in the war. After some success and serious wounds, he rose in rank to major general (2 stars).

---

[17] Magnanimous is the more common adjective form of the noun magnanimity. To be magnanimous means to be generous in forgiving injury or insult.
Prostrate: lying face down or in a vulnerable position.

(4) In 1835, Scott wrote *Infantry Tactics, Or, Rules for the Exercise and Maneuvre of the United States Infantry* in three volumes. This became the standard drill manual for the army for the next century.

(5) General Scott served in the Black Hawk War, the Second Seminole War, and the Creek War of 1836.

(6) General Scott was assigned to supervise removal of the Cherokee to Indian Territory in 1838. He is credited with some attempts to implement the removal in a humane manner, though these efforts were not extensive. Scott was concerned with humane treatment. However, he proved to be more concerned with executing the order.

(7) In 1841 General Scott was appointed Commanding General of the US Army, a position he held for the next twenty years.

(8) During the Mexican War, Winfield Scott was assigned with the capturing Mexico City. He landed his army at Vera Cruz and marched it directly westward.[18] On this march, Captain Robert E. Lee was the engineer charged with planning the tricky route inland, and Lee performed well. Scott's army was resisted by that of Santa Anna in route and won victories all along the way.

(9) When Scott's army reached Mexico City it was outnumbered 2-to-1, but Santa Anna proved to be an ineffective military leader and the Mexican forces were defeated in an intensive house-to-house struggle. The capture of Mexico City ended the war. Throughout the entire campaign, Scott had outmaneuvered Santa Anna at every turn.

(10) General Scott earned the title "Old Fuss and Feathers" by his insistence on perfectly pressed and cleaned uniforms with brass and shoes shined.

(11) Winfield Scott was nominated for President by the Whig Party in 1852, but lost the election to Franklin Pierce.

(12) When the Civil War began, President Lincoln asked Commanding General Scott to design a plan to win the war. Scott proposed to blockade the South and take control of the Mississippi River in order to sever Texas and part of Louisiana from the other Southern states while stopping the flow of Southern commerce

---

[18] This is the same route taken by Hernan Cortes in 1519.

and military supplies on the river. With these measures, Scott assured the President that the war could be won in three years.

Lincoln rejected the plan. With the Confederate capital of Richmond less than 100 miles from Washington, DC, Lincoln wanted a plan to capture Richmond within weeks and end the war quickly. The Northern press agreed with Lincoln and scoffed at Scott's plan, which they compared to a long snake. The Anaconda Plan, they called it.

Having been rebuffed, General Scott resigned from the army. The Union Navy blockaded the South, cutting off vital supplies and stopping the export of cotton. General Grant and Admiral Farragut seized control of the Mississippi. And the South was brought to surrender, not in three years as Scott had predicted, but in four.

Quotes from Winfield Scott

My politics are of a practical kind – the integrity of the country, the supremacy of the Federal government, an honorable peace, or none at all.

I placed the Marines where the hardest work was to be accomplished, and I never once found my confidence in them misplaced.

The enemy say that Americans are good at a long shot, but cannot stand the cold iron. I call upon you instantly to give a lie to this slander. Charge!

Brigham Young (1801-1877) and the Latter Day Saints

(1)   In 1830 Joseph Smith published *The Book of Mormon* which he said he had been led to after having visions of Jesus and an angel. Smith said that the book had been written on gold tablets in an obscure language and buried in New York State. According to Smith, God allowed him to translate the tablets. Smith then founded the Church of Jesus Christ of Latter Day Saint, also known as the Mormon religion.

(2)   Brigham Young was among the early converts to the new religion of Latter Day Saints and became a prominent leader.

(3)   Members of Joseph Smith's early Mormon Church lived in a single community and came into conflict with majority non-Mormons everywhere they went mainly because one of their customs was polygamy. A man could have any number of wives. The Mormons were also thought to be a political threat because they voted as a block and shared communal enterprises.

(4)   Joseph Smith was murdered in Nauvoo, Illinois in 1844, and Brigham Young took over leadership of the LDS community.

(5)   Brigham Young led the Mormon community to the region of the Great Salt Lake in 1847. At the time, this was still part of New Mexico Territory under the claim of Mexico. The site was chosen by Young because he believed that it was so desolate that no other group would be interested in settling there.

(6)   The year after the Mormons came to Salt Lake, the region came under US control as the entire New Mexico Territory was awarded to the US by the terms of the Treaty of Guadalupe-Hidalgo which ended the Mexican War.

(7)   As part of the US, the Salt Lake region became the part of Territory of Utah, which included present day Nevada and parts of other present day states. Brigham Young was appointed Governor of the territory and Superintendent of Indian Affairs.

(8)   Salt Lake City, the community founded by Brigham Young, is now the headquarters of the world Mormon Church and the capital of Utah.

(9) Mormon leaders envisioned the great state of Deseret encompassing, not only Utah Territory, but also much of present day Arizona and Southern California. Under Brigham Young, Mormons were sent out to establish communities throughout the southwest.

(10) The Mormons, under Brigham Young, came into conflict with some of their indigenous neighbors. They also had conflicts with the US government and Anglo settlers, who were mostly crossing Utah with no intention of settling there. One party of settlers heading through Utah came into conflict with the Mormons in 1857 and were attacked and massacred (the Mountain Meadows Massacre). Most Mormons believe that Brigham Young was not involved in this. The evidence is unclear.

When President James Buchanan decided to replace Young with a non-Mormon governor and sent his choice for governor out to Utah with a contingent of federal troops, Young, at first, directed a military resistance which lasted a year and became known as the Mormon War. When Young relented and allowed the new governor to take charge, he was pardoned of charges stemming from the resistance.

(11) Brigham Young was a man of his time, constrained by the narrow vision of his time. He believed in slavery and excluded black people from being clergy in the LDS Church.

(12) In 1875 Brigham Young founded Brigham Young University, which is owned entirely by the LDS Church.

(13) Steve Young, former All-Pro quarterback and one time Most Valuable NFL player with the San Francisco Forty-niners, is a direct descendent of Brigham Young.

Quotes by Brigham Young

True independence and freedom can only exist in doing what's right.

Love the giver more than the gift.

Education is the power to think clearly, the power to act well in the worlds work, and the power to appreciate life.

A good man, is a good man, whether in this church, or out of it.

We should never permit ourselves to do anything that we are not willing to see our children do.

Remember, a chip on the shoulder is a sure sign of wood higher up.

It is wise for us to forget our troubles, there are always new ones to replace them.

CHAPTER 5

SLAVERY, RESISTANCE AND COMPROMISE, 1848-1860

Traditionally, American history teachers are fond of saying that the American Civil War had three causes: (1) a dispute over tariffs; (2) the issue of states' rights versus the power of the federal government, including the right to withdraw from the Union; and (3) slavery. This allows us to believe that the soldiers of the Confederacy were fighting for some noble cause, and no doubt the volunteers felt this to be true. But in actuality, the tariff dispute could easily have been worked out and was seldom debated as an issue after 1840, and the states' rights argument was concentrated on the "rights" of the states to have slavery supported by the nation in terms of fugitive slave laws, muzzling critics, and extending slavery into new territories.

The strongest argument proposed to justify the southern cause is the right to withdraw from the Union. This is what many Confederates thought they were fighting for. President Lincoln convinced Union soldiers that they were fighting to preserve the Union. Poor whites in the South would not have fought to preserve slavery, and poor whites in the north would have been unwilling to risk their lives to end it. But the overarching fact is that if slavery had not existed in America no civil war would have occurred. The war could not end with Union victory and slavery intact.

Opposition to slavery among some Anglo-Americans was not new in the years immediately preceding the Civil War. The words of Thomas Jefferson in the Declaration of Independence inspired Northern states to outlaw slavery shortly after the American Revolution, and there was a brief trend at that time for slave owners to set their slaves free. But Anglo-Americans feared being overwhelmed by large numbers of free blacks. This led to the formation of The American Colonization Society in 1816, which resettled former slaves in a new country called Liberia in Africa. Beginning in the 1830s, a small number of vocal opponents of slavery focused on the issue. By this time, slavery had been confined to only the southern states. Anti-slavery proponents insisted that slavery not be extended into the western territories and worked for its total abolition. Pro-slavery southerners were angry that the rest of the country seemed to be working to extinguish their way of life.

Resistance to slavery in the antebellum years involved many players and took many forms.[19]

Escaped slave Harriet Tubman led others to escape. Escaped slave Frederick Douglass forcefully denounced slavery to Northern audiences. William Lloyd Garrison used the power of the press. Harriet Beecher Stowe also wrote. The Grimke sisters, who had grown up in a slave holding southern family, wrote and spoke of the evils of slavery. Henry David Thoreau developed a theory for civil disobedience. And John Brown chose violence, which was a major cause of polarization and hatred, while Henry Clay tried unceasingly to create compromise between the North and the South.

Harriet Tubman (1822-1913), Moses

(1) Harriet Tubman, an escaped slave, made repeated trips into Maryland to aid others to escape slavery. She connected with the "underground railroad," a system of safe-houses aiding escaped slaves. As a "conductor" on this railroad, Tubman boasted later that she never lost a passenger. The total number of African-Americans rescued by Harriet Tubman is believed to have been approximately 300.

(2) Harriet Tubman was born a slave in Maryland in 1822.

---

[19] Antebellum: the literal meaning is "before the war." In US history it means the years immediately preceding the Civil War, about 1848 to 1861.

(3)   Tubman stood 5 feet tall.

(4)   Harriet Tubman received a head wound as a young girl from a heavy metal object thrown by her "owner." The injury continued to bother her throughout her life.

(5)   Tubman escaped to Philadelphia in 1849.

(6)   Shortly after her own escape, Tubman returned to Maryland to help her family escape.

(7)   As the radical abolitionist John Brown was organizing his troops, he attempted to enlist Harriet Tubman as a logistical aide calling her "General Tubman."

(8)   During the Civil War, Tubman served the Union cause as a guide, nurse, and spy in the South. She was granted a pension in her old age for her service in the war.

(9)   In her later years, Harriet Tubman joined the suffragist movement advocating voting rights for women.

Quote from Harriet Tubman

Every great dream begins with a dreamer. Always remember, you have within you the strength, the patience, and the passion to reach for the stars to change the world.

William Lloyd Garrison (1805-1879) and *The Liberator*

(1)   William Lloyd Garrison began his own weekly newspaper, *The Liberator*, in 1831, clearly indicating that the only purpose of the paper was the complete abolition of slavery. The paper continued without interruption until slavery was abolished by the passage of the Thirteenth Amendment in 1865.

(2)   William Lloyd Garrison grew-up poor in Massachusetts after his father left in 1808. He did odd jobs as a child to help support the family.

(3)   Garrison began work in the newspaper business as an apprentice at the age of 13.

(4) Garrison briefly joined the American Colonization Society, an organization dedicated to relocating former slaves to Liberia in Africa. But Garrison's main interest was in freeing slaves, while other members were mostly interested in reducing the number of free black Africans in America.

(5) Before he established *The Liberator*, Garrison had worked as co-editor of the Quaker newspaper *Genius of Universal Emancipation* in Baltimore.

(6) Garrison was quick to expose and embarrass those involved in the slave trade, even if the involvement was only slight. While working on the Baltimore newspaper, he was convicted of slander and ordered to pay a $50 fine. He refuse and spent seven weeks in jail. He left Baltimore soon after.

(7) In 1832 Garrison organized the New England Anti-Slavery Society which soon became the American Anti-Slavery Society.

(8) The violent, bloody slave rebellion of Nat Turner occurred months after Garrison began the publication of *The Liberator*. Because of this coincidence, some southerners blamed the rebellion on provocation by Garrison's paper. He was a wanted criminal in South Carolina, and Georgia offered a $5000 reward for anyone who could deliver him to the state for trial.

(9) In 1835 Garrison was attacked and subdued by a Boston mob, which intended to tar and feather him. He was rescued by the Boston mayor, who intervened by arresting Garrison.

(10) By 1840 Garrison had also begun advocating for women's rights.

(11) As part of his anti-slavery work, Garrison recruited articulate Africans, especially escaped slaves, as speakers. The escaped slave, Frederick Douglass, was recruited by Garrison, and Garrison helped promote and protect Douglass.

Quotes from William Lloyd Garrison

I am in earnest - I will not equivocate - I will not excuse - I will not retreat a single inch - and I will be heard!

Are right and wrong convertible terms, dependent upon popular opinion?

That which is not just is not law.

Frederick Douglass (1818-1895) and *The North Star*

(1)   Frederick Douglass was born a slave in Maryland. He did not know who his white father was. As a young man, he escaped slavery by going north with the help of a free black woman whom he married shortly after.

(2)   Douglass was recruited to speak for the anti-slavery abolitionist movement shortly after his arrival in the north.[20]

(3)   Douglass had learned to read with the help of his master's wife while he was a slave.

(4)   As a slave, Douglass acted as a preacher in a slave church where he attempted to teach other slaves to read the Bible until this was discovered by the slave owners.

(5)   Douglass was so articulate when speaking against slavery in the North that some people said that he must be lying; he could not have been raised as a slave. To prove that he was telling the truth, Douglass published his autobiography, *A Narrative of the Life of Frederick Douglass, an American Slave*. Then he went to England to avoid being returned to slavery. While he was in England, white friends raised money to purchase Douglass' freedom from his Maryland master.

(6)   Douglass eventually published his own anti-slavery newspaper, *The North Star*. (The North Star was known to be the object in the night sky which fugitive slaves followed to escape to the north.)

(7)   Douglass was among the earliest supporters of equal rights (and the right to vote) for women. He was the only African-American to speak at the famous Seneca Falls Women's Convention of 1848.

---

[20] Abolition (the root word is abolish which means to do away with completely). The abolitionists were people, mostly in the North, who were working to do away with slavery in the United States.

Eloquence: extreme skill, precision, and/or beauty.

(8) Abolitionist John Brown visited Douglass only two months before staging his famous raid on Harper's Ferry. Douglass advised Brown against the plan.

(9) During the Civil War, Douglass strongly encouraged President Lincoln to allow African-Americans to serve in the Union Army. Beginning in 1863 (after the Emancipation Proclamation), African-Americans were finally allowed to enlist. By the end of the war, 170,000 African-Americans were serving or had served in the US military. This number is large enough to suggest that the participation of African-Americans was a major factor in the eventual Union victory. Douglass asserted that by their participation in the war, African-Americans had earned the right to full citizenship.

(10) A minor political party, the Equal Rights Party, nominated a woman, Victoria Woodhull, for US President and Frederick Douglass for Vice-president in 1872.

(11) In later years, Douglass served as US charge d'afffairs (ambassador) to the Dominican Republic and US Marshal for the District of Columbia.

(12) Douglass continued to advocate for equal rights for African-Americans and women until his death in 1895.

(13) Frederick Douglass wrote a later autobiography, *The Life and Times of Frederick Douglass*. It was first published in 1881, then revised in 1892 (only 3 years before his death).

Quotes from Frederick Douglass

If there is no struggle, there is no progress.

People might not get all they work for in this world, but they must certainly work for all they get.

A little learning, indeed, may be a dangerous thing, but the want of learning is a calamity to any people.

Henry Clay (1777-1852), The Great Compromiser

(1) Henry Clay, a career politician, gained the epithet "the Great Compromiser" by taking the lead in negotiating three major compromises between the Northern States and the South which kept the Union together for 40 years.

(2) Henry Clay was born in Virginia in 1777. He descended from some of the earliest Virginia settlers.

(3) Henry Clay's father, John Clay, a Baptist minister, who owned a small plantation with 22 slaves, died when the boy was only four years old.

(4) Henry Clay moved to Kentucky in 1797 and began practicing law.

(5) Clay and his wife, Lucretia had six children, five of whom died before their parents. Four daughters died very young. Whooping cough, yellow fever, and complications of child birth were causes. One son, Henry Clay, Jr., died in the Mexican War at the Battle of Buena Vista.

(6) In 1805 Henry Clay became a professor at Transylvania University in Lexington, Kentucky.

(7) In 1806 Clay and his legal partner successfully defended Aaron Burr in his famous treason trial.

(8) While Clay was a slave owner all his life, as a young man entering Kentucky politics, he advocated abolition of slavery in his state.

(9) In 1806 the Kentucky state legislature elected Henry Clay to fill a brief, temporary vacancy in the US Senate. Clay had his first experience in national government, serving as a US Senator for two months. He was not yet 30 years old, officially too young to serve in the Senate.

(10) In 1807 Henry Clay was elected Speaker of the Kentucky House of Representatives.

(11) In 1810, Clay was chosen once again to fill a temporary vacancy in the US Senate. He served for one year this time.

(12) While completing his one year in the US Senate, Henry Clay decided to run for the US House of Representatives, and was elected easily.

(13) The newly elected member of the House of Representatives from Kentucky, Henry Clay, was already a leader of the "War Hawks," those Senators and Representative advocating war with Great Britain. He was unhappy with British support for indigenous resistance on the frontier, and he was also an expansionist and may have seen war as an opportunity to invade Canada and add it to the Union.

(14) As a popular leader of the War Hawks with many connections due to his previous service in the Senate, Clay was elected Speaker of the House on his first day.

(15) Henry Clay was a member of the American delegation in peace talks to end the War of 1812. During the negotiations he frequently found himself at odds with fellow American negotiator, John Quincy Adams. The peace treaty, the Treaty of Ghent, was signed on December 25, 1814.

(16) Beginning around 1816, Congressman Clay began advocating what he called "the American System." Its three major components were: tariffs to protect American industry and raise revenue; internal construction of roads and canals to link the country together; and a Bank of the United States to insure currency stability. (Ironically, Clay had been instrumental in killing the first Bank of the United States.)

(17) Henry Clay was among the founders of the American Colonization Society, an organization which worked to facilitate the colonization of Liberia in Africa by former slaves. The group feared a large number of free black Africans in American cities.

(18) In 1820 as Speaker of the House, Henry Clay designed the first of the three compromises between the North and the South with which he is credited. Missouri had applied for admission into the Union as a slave state. At that time, there were an equal number of slave states and free states. The admission of Missouri would tip the balance in the Senate.

By the terms of the Missouri Compromise, Missouri was admitted as a slave state. Maine, which had been part of Massachusetts, became a separate free state. So the balance in the Senate was maintained.

It was also agreed that no other slave states would be created out of the Louisiana Territory north of 36° 30' north latitude.

(19) In 1824 Henry Clay made the first of his three unsuccessful bids for the Presidency. In a field of four candidates, Clay finished last and did not win a single electoral vote. Andrew Jackson outpolled his rivals by a considerable margin, but Jackson did not have the Electoral College majority (50%) needed for outright victory. As prescribed in the Constitution, the election was deferred to the House of Representatives where Henry Clay was the Speaker. Clay withdrew from the contest, while throwing his support behind John Quincy Adams, and Adams was elected.

When Adams took office, he appointed Clay as Secretary of State. This led to the famous accusation of "the corrupt bargain of 1824."

(20) Clay was elected to his first full term in the Senate in 1830.

(21) Henry Clay sponsored a bill to re-charter the Bank of the United States, which he knew President Jackson would veto, and Jackson did. The purpose of the bill seems to have been to give Clay an issue on which to run for President against Jackson in 1832. Clay was nominated by the new Whig (anti-Jackson) Party. Jackson won the election easily.

(22) In 1833 South Carolina had claimed the right to nullify a federal law and threated to secede from the Union. President Jackson had threatened to lead the army into South Carolina himself and hang every secessionist. Then Henry Clay sponsored the "Compromise Tariff of 1833," which lowered the tariff rate on manufactured goods enough to appease the south without angering northern manufacturers. Clay had the support of John C. Calhoun and Daniel Webster in convincing Congress to approve the compromise bill.

(23) In 1844 Henry Clay ran for President for the third time. He was defeated by Democrat, James K. Polk. Clay is famous for having said, "I'd rather be right than President."

(24) As southern leaders were upset about lack of support from the north in apprehending escaped slaves and again threatening secession, and California was in chaos with the discovery of gold before a solid territorial government could be established, Henry Clay sponsored the "Compromise of 1850." The main provisions of the compromise were that California would be admitted to the Union as a free state, and a tough Fugitive Slave Law would guarantee that northerners would assist in returning escaped slaves to their owners. During the period 1820 to 1850, three major compromises had kept the Union together; all were sponsored by Henry Clay, "the Great Compromiser."

The Fugitive Slave Law of 1850, however, drove the north and the south farther apart in the long run. It was unenforceable and it created resentment in both camps. People in the north resented it because it put a heavy burden upon them to aid in return of fugitive slaves when northerners either had no interest in this or opposed it. Southerners became resentful because they thought they had a deal and felt deceived when the law was ignored.

Quotes from Henry Clay

I have heard something said about allegiance to the South. I know no South, no North, no East, no West, to which I owe any allegiance.

Government is a trust, and the officers of the government are trustees. And both the trust and the trustees are created for the benefit of the people.

Of all the properties which belong to honorable men, not one is so highly prized as that of character.

Statistics are no substitute for judgment.

An oppressed people are authorized whenever they can to rise and break their fetters.

If you wish to avoid foreign collision, you had better abandon the ocean.

Henry David Thoreau (1817-1862) and Transcendentalism

(1) Henry David Thoreau was born in Concord, Massachusetts to a family of modest means. His father was a pencil maker. Henry David would become one the greatest intellectual leaders of the nineteenth century.

(2) HD Thoreau graduated from Harvard 1837.

(3) Thoreau became a protégé and close person friend on Ralph Waldo Emerson.[21] Eventually the two became the acknowledged leaders of the Transcendentalist movement. The movement emphasized the inherent goodness of all people and nature, the corrupting influence of society, and the virtue of self-reliance.

(4) As an experiment in the virtue of self-reliance, Thoreau abandoned civilization and went off into the woods around Walden Pond. There he built his own house and attempted to live a self-sustaining life, as he took notes on his experiences and thoughts. Thoreau's experiment lasted two years, two months, and two days. The result is the classic book *Walden*, which describes his life during that time and is interspersed with inspiration and wisdom. *Walden* is considered to be one of the greatest books of American literature.

(5) Thoreau continued to work at his family's pencil business, and developed new, more efficient processes for the manufacture of pencils.

(6) Thoreau participated in the Underground Railroad, helping slaves escape to freedom, and he condemned the Fugitive Slave Act of 1850.

(7) In 1846 Thoreau was jailed for a day for refusing to pay taxes. He was disgusted that slavery still existed in the United States and that the Mexican War had been provoked to steal California from Mexico. There is a story that Emerson came to see him in jail as soon as he heard about the situation. In their encounter, Emerson supposedly asked, "What are you doing in there?"

---

[21] Protégé: a person guided or helped in his or her career by another person.

to which Thoreau supposedly reply "That's not the important question. The important question is 'What are you doing out there?'" Some anonymous person paid the taxes for Thoreau, and he was released the next day.

(8) After Thoreau's brief protest and night in jail, he wrote a now famous essay, "On the Duty of Civil Disobedience." It is available as a short book. This book became the inspiration and model for operations for Mohandas Gandhi, Martin Luther King, and Nelson Mandela.

(9) Thoreau knew the radical abolitionist John Brown personally. When Brown was captured at Harper's Ferry, Thoreau spoke openly in defense of Brown, comparing Brown to Jesus Christ, and asserting his own support for the abolition of slavery.

Quotes from Henry David Thoreau

It's not what you look at that matters, it's what you see.

Friends... they cherish one another's hopes.

They are kind to one another's dreams.

This world is but a canvas to our imagination.

The language of friendship is not words but meanings.

Many men go fishing all of their lives without knowing that it is not fish they are after.

You must live in the present, launch yourself on every wave, find your eternity in each moment.

True friendship can afford true knowledge. It does not depend on darkness and ignorance.

Pursue some path, however narrow and crooked, in which you can walk with love and reverence.

Wealth is the ability to fully experience life.

It is not enough to be busy. So are the ants. The question is: What are we busy about?

What lies behind us and what lies ahead of us are tiny matters compared to what lies within us.

If a man does not keep pace with his companions, perhaps it is because he hears a different drummer. Let him step to the music which he hears, however measured or far away.

Never look back unless you are planning to go that way.

Success usually comes to those who are too busy to be looking for it.

If the machine of government is of such a nature that it requires you to be the agent of injustice to another, then, I say, break the law.

Live your beliefs and you can turn the world around.

If you have built castles in the air, your work need not be lost; that is where they should be. Now put the foundations under them.

Aim above morality. Be not simply good, be good for something.

Harriet Beecher Stowe (1811-1896)

(1) In 1858 Harriet Beecher Stowe published one of the most influential novels in American history.

(2) Harriet Beecher was born in Litchfield, Connecticut. She was the seventh of 13 children. Her father was Lyman Beecher, a Calvinist minister.

(3) One of Harriet's sisters was Catherine Beecher, a noted author and educator.

(4) One of Harriet's brothers was Henry Ward Beecher, a well-known abolitionist preacher.

(5) Harriet was educated at the Hartford Female Seminary, which was run by her sister, Catherine.

(6) At the age of 21 Harriet moved to Cincinnati, Ohio to live with her father, Lyman, who had become president of the Lane Theological Seminary there.

(7) In Cincinnati, Harriet met and married Calvin Stowe, a professor at her father's seminary.

(8) Cincinnati was directly across the Ohio River from the slave state of Kentucky and had a significant black African population. The Stowes observed racial tensions in the city and some of the effects of slavery.

(9) Cincinnati was an important point on the Underground Railroad that assisted slaves attempting to escape. Calvin and Harriett Stowe took an active part in the Underground Railroad.

(10) Harriet Beecher Stowe was a prolific author. She published more than 30 books in her lifetime.

(11) After years in Cincinnati, Calvin and Harriet Stowe moved to Brunswick, Maine, for Calvin to teach at Bowdoin College.

(12) While in Maine, Harriet wrote her only famous novel, *Uncle Tom's Cabin*, which shed a bad light on slavery. The novel was widely distributed in the north and banned in most of the south. The effect in the north was to make many readers more sympathetic to the plight of slaves. In the south, the book elicited rage. Stowe had not lived in the south, so she knew nothing about slavery and the south, it was argued. The reaction among all Americans was so strong that when President Lincoln met Stowe for the first time during the Civil War he remarked that he was happy to meet the lady who started this war.

Quotes from Harriet Beecher Stowe

Never give up, for that is just the place and time that the tide will turn.

The bitterest tears shed over graves are for words left unsaid and deeds left undone.

Perhaps it is impossible for a person who does no good to do no harm.

John Brown (1800-1859), Devil or Warrior

(1) John Brown is included in this book because he is a larger than life figure without whom the Civil War story cannot be told completely. He is also the most controversial "hero" included in this book. He was involved in the savage execution and mutilation of five men at Pottawatomie Creek in Kansas with thin provocation.

(2) The Kansas-Nebraska Act of 1854 had opened Kansas to the possibility of slavery. Pro-slavery and anti-slavery supporters flooded into Kansas, each group hoping to win the new state to its side. Conflict arose. That conflict turned violent in 1856 after members of the pro-slavery faction sacked the anti-slavery town of Lawrence, destroying property, but killing no one. In retaliation, John Brown led the raid on Pottawatomie. The vicious killings there precipitated violence which continued right up to the Civil War, and Kansas became known as "Bleeding Kansas."

(3) In New Richmond, Pennsylvania, between 1820 and 1832, John Brown had raised cattle, helped establish a post office, and operated a tannery, which employed 15 people.

(4) John Brown moved to Franklin Mills, Ohio in 1836. His tannery there ran into financial difficulty during the financial "Panic of 1837" and he declared bankruptcy.

(5) When the Reverend Elijah P. Lovejoy, an abolitionist newspaper publisher, was murdered in 1837, Brown vowed to "consecrate my life to the destruction of slavery."

(6) John Brown was deeply religious and saw his anti-slavery work as inspired by God.

(7) John Brown had 20 children. His sons were the core of his followers during his anti-slavery activities.

(8) In 1859 John Brown led a raid on the US Army arsenal at Harper's Ferry, Virginia. His plan was to seize the guns and ammunition and continue from there through the south, inciting slave rebellion and enlisting rebellious slaves to join his army. Brown's group did take possession of the armory, but they found themselves surrounded by federal troops under Colonel Robert E. Lee. Brown was wounded in the siege and forced to surrender. This raid had the effect of shocking all Americans. The southern states began organizing militias in case something like this would occur again. These militias would provide a nucleus for the Confederate Army.

Attitudes in both the north and the south were hardened by John Brown's raid.

(9) John Brown received a speedy trial. From the time of his apprehension to the time of his execution, only six weeks had elapsed. On the day of his execution, John Brown prepared a written statement in which he said

> I, John Brown, am now quite certain that the crimes of this guilty land will never be purged away but with blood. I had, as I now think, vainly flattered myself that without very much bloodshed it might be done.

(10) At the time of his execution John Brown was praised by many, including Henry David Thoreau and Ralph Waldo Emerson. Victor Hugo made a plea for clemency for Brown. But Lincoln called him insane and William Lloyd Garrison said that Brown was "sadly misguided."

(11) During the Civil War, the song "John Brown's Body" was composed and sung by Union soldiers to the tune of "The Battle Hymn of the Republic."

(12) The impact of John Brown upon the Civil War is highly debatable. It can be argued that he provided the impetus which caused the

Civil War by heating up the anger on both sides. Without John Brown, it can be argued, civil war might have been averted, but this is doubtful. It can also be argued that the fear inspired by John Brown in 1859 which cause the southern states to establish strong militias, resulted in the South being well prepared for war. Without John Brown, perhaps the South might have been defeated more easily and much sooner.

Quotes from John Brown

Now, if it is deemed necessary that I should forfeit my life for the furtherance of the ends of justice, and mingle my blood further with the blood of my children, and with the blood of millions in this slave country whose rights are disregarded by wicked, cruel, and unjust enactments, I submit: so let it be done!

I cannot remember a night so dark as to have hindered the coming day.

Be mild with the mild, shrewd with the crafty, confiding to the honest, rough to the ruffian, and a thunderbolt to the liar. But in all this, never be unmindful of your own dignity.

CHAPTER 6

THE CIVIL WAR, 1861-1865

The Civil War lasted for four full years. More than 600,000 American men died in the war, and the South was left devastated. Many Americans seem to want to honor those who fought by inventing reasons for the war which did not exist. It is true that Confederate soldiers thought they were fighting for states' rights, and Union soldier were convinced that they were fighting to preserve the Union (at least until Lincoln issued the Emancipation Proclamation). The simple overriding fact is that if slavery had not existed, there would not have been a civil war. Well intended self-deception does no honor to the dead, but it can perpetuate the mistakes of the past.

To be completely fair to the sons and daughters of the South, the doctrine of nullification (the right of a state to nullify a federal law) was first purported by Thomas Jefferson in the Kentucky Resolution of 1798, and the right of secession from the Union was suggested by leaders of New England (northern) colonies at the Hartford Convention in 1814. Neither nullification nor secession was a completely settled issue in 1861. Southerners can argue that if all Federal troops had been withdrawn from the South and the South had been allowed to secede, the blood bath of 1861-1865 might have been avoided. The brutal abomination of slavery would still have to face a reckoning, but slavery was far from the minds of poor Southern soldiers in 1861. The South was invaded by an outside force. Men in wartime flock to the service of their country without thought of whether their country is right or wrong, especially when their country is under direct attack.

The immediate trigger for the war was the election of the Republican, Lincoln, to the presidency with less than 40% of the popular vote. Many, including Lincoln, expected a short war, but the South was fighting a defensive war, not dissimilar to the American Revolution. As vastly more powerful British had not been able to defeat the Americans, so too, the more powerful North struggled to invade and defeat the South. A turning point of the war came with the defeat of the Confederates under Robert E. Lee at Gettysburg and the simultaneous capture of Vicksburg, which gave the Union full control of the Mississippi. The killing blows were delivered in 1864 by US Grant and William Tecumseh Sherman as they waged unrelenting "total war" to force the Confederate surrender.

Abraham Lincoln (1809-1865) and the Republican Party

(1)   Abraham Lincoln was born in a one room log cabin in Kentucky and largely self-educated. As a young man, he moved to Illinois, where he made his political career.

(2)   Abraham Lincoln's parents belonged to the Separatist Baptist Church, which forbade slavery.

(3)   In 1842 Abraham Lincoln married Mary Todd, the daughter of a wealthy slave holding family in Kentucky.

(4)   Abraham and Mary Lincoln had four sons. Only one lived to adulthood.

(5)   All his life, Abraham Lincoln suffered from bouts of depression.

(6)   Lincoln served as a captain in the Illinois militia during the Black Hawk War of 1832, but saw very little action.

(7)   In his early career, Lincoln served as postmaster and later county surveyor in New Salem, Illinois after running unsuccessfully twice for local offices.

(8)   In 1834 Lincoln won his first elected position, a seat in the Illinois state legislature.

(9)   After studying entirely on his own, Lincoln was admitted to the Illinois bar in 1836. The Lincolns then moved to Springfield,

Illinois, where Abraham began his law practice and continued to serve in the state legislature.

(10) Lincoln, running as a Whig candidate, was defeated in his first run for the US House of Representatives. But was elected on his second try in 1846. He served one two year term. This was Abraham Lincoln's only service as an official in the national government before he became President.

(11) Lincoln was serving in the House of Representatives during the Mexican War. He opposed the war, seeing it as an artificially created land grab by President Polk. As a protest, Lincoln sponsored the "Spot Resolution" by which he challenged the President to show him the spot on the map where "American blood has been shed on American soil."

(12) Abraham Lincoln held no government office from 1849 through 1861, but focused on building up his law practice. He did, however, run for US Senate in 1858.

(13) In 1854 Senator Stephen A. Douglas of Illinois, a rising star in the Democratic Party with an eye on the Presidency, sponsored the Kansas-Nebraska Act, which opened the door to statehood for those two territories with the provision that each new state would decide whether it would be slave or free based on a vote of the people (popular sovereignty).

This would be the first time since 1820 that territories north of the Missouri Compromise line of 36°30' north latitude would be open to slavery. Angry northern reaction to this act led to the creation of the Republican Party. The Republican Party was composed of a coalition of people who opposed the extension of slavery into the western territories of the United States. The coalition included: (1) farmers who did not want to compete with the slave system in the territories, (2) abolitionist who wanted to end slavery altogether, and (3) others with other motivations. Lincoln joined the party based on his opposition to the extension of slavery into the territories. He was not an abolitionist, though he was sure that slavery was morally wrong. He thought that it could be limited, and it would then die out on its own.

(14) Lincoln came into national prominence through his unsuccessful run for US Senate in 1858. Running now as a Republican, Lincoln was opposing the Democratic incumbent, the nationally known "Little Giant," Stephen A. Douglas, who had infuriated opponents of the extension of slavery with his Kansas-Nebraska Act.

Lincoln, who had no real chance of defeating the popular Douglas, challenge him to a series of debates. Douglas accepted, and reports of the debates made news over the entire country. By holding his own in these debates with Douglas, Lincoln propelled himself into the leadership of the Republican Party.

(15) In 1860 the acknowledged leader of the Republican Party was William Seward. He expected to be nominated by his party for President. But Seward was an abolitionist and many party members were not. Lincoln won the party's nomination because he was considered to be a moderate who could appeal to all Republicans. He was opposed to any extension of slavery into the territories, but he did not openly advocate abolition.

(16) Stephen A. Douglas, the Democratic nominee for President in 1860, had made a statement in the course of the Lincoln-Douglas debates of 1858 which caused southerners to distrust his commitment to the cause of slavery. The Southern Democrats put forth their own candidate, while threatening to secede from the Union if Lincoln were elected. In the midst of an impending crisis, a new party, the Unionist, nominated another candidate.

With the vote split among four candidates, Abraham Lincoln was able to win the majority of the vote in the Electoral College, though he had less than 40% of the popular vote and he did not win a single electoral vote in the South. He had not even been on the ballot in most Southern states.

(17) In reaction to the election of the Republican, Lincoln, South Carolina seceded from the Union. Six other slave states followed

suit in the interim while James Buchanan was still the President. Eventually eleven states seceded.

(18) While Lincoln was on the way to his 1861 inauguration, an assassination plot was discovered and thwarted in Baltimore. With tensions running high, President-elect Lincoln allowed the security services to sneak him into Washington, DC for the inauguration.

(19) The Civil War began when Confederate forces fired on Fort Sumter in Charleston harbor in April 1861. President Lincoln had announced in his inaugural speech that he would not be the aggressor. If civil war came, it would be initiated by the South.

(20) President Lincoln moved quickly to prevent further defections from the Union. Keeping the slave state of Maryland in the Union was critical, because Washington, DC is located between Maryland and Virginia. If Maryland joined the Confederacy, the US capital would be in the middle of Confederate territory. Even with Maryland remaining in the Union, the threat of spies in Maryland undermining the Union was constant during the war.

Lincoln imposed martial law in Maryland, a move in clear violation of the Constitution. When questioned about the decision, Lincoln replied that it would make no sense to save the Constitution and lose the Union.

Four slave "border states" stayed in the Union: Maryland, Kentucky, Missouri, and West Virginia, which actually broke away from Virginia when the rest of the state joined the Confederacy.

(21) The Civil War on land was basically two wars. In the east, the capital of the United States was only 100 miles north of the capital of the Confederate States of America. The Grand Army of the Potomac, protecting Washington, DC, faced the Army of Northern Virginia, defending Richmond. Lincoln and many others believed that a quick strike south could capture Richmond and win the war. "On to Richmond" was the battle cry of the Army of the Potomac.

In the west, the war was not as locally defined, but capture and control of the Mississippi River by the Union would make shipping difficult for the Confederacy.

The Union had tremendous advantages—more people, more industry, and a navy. The Union navy was able to blockade the South, cutting off both exports of cotton and imports of supplies.

The one big advantage that the Confederacy had was that their troops did not need to invade the North to win.

Despite the advantages that the Union side had, the war went badly for them in the first year, beginning with a humiliating defeat at Bull Run.

(22) The Army of Northern Virginia, under General Robert E. Lee, invaded Maryland in 1862 in an attempt to inflict enough damage to sway public opinion in the North against the war. These invaders were met by the Army of the Potomac under General George McClellan at Antietam. The bloody battle that was fought there saw the largest number of casualties of any one day battle in the entire Civil War. Almost 3000 soldiers were killed that day. Total casualties were more than 22,000. The Union lost slightly more men than the Confederates, but Lee broke off the battle and retreated back across the Potomac River into Virginia.

Asserting that Lee had been forced back to Virginia, Lincoln claimed a victory, and followed up with the preliminary Emancipation Proclamation on September 22, 1862. This was a threat to the South that the slaves in any state which remained in rebellion after January 1, 1863 would be forever freed.

(23) Based on his authority as Commander-in-Chief, Lincoln issued the actual Emancipation Proclamation on January 1, 1863. It did not free all the slaves. The freedom granted was for slaves in the states in rebellion. It did not include the slaves in the border states of Maryland, Missouri, Kentucky, and West Virginia. In

practical terms the Proclamation freed few slaves, because it could not be enforced without Union control in the South.

What the Proclamation did do was to inspire slaves to escape to the North and aid the Union cause. It also opened the door for recruitment of black Africans into the Union army. By the end of the war 170,000 black Africans were or had been in Union uniform, helping to win their own freedom.

The Proclamation also forced the issue of slavery along. If the Union were to win the war, the slaves in all the former Confederate states would be free. This would put pressure on the Border States to free their slaves also.

(24) The battle which most turned the tide of the war was the Battle of Gettysburg in the summer of 1863. This was also the largest single battle of the war. Union casualties totaled 23,000 with more than 3000 dead. A section of the battlefield was made into a cemetery for the Union soldiers who died there.

On November 19, 1863, President Abraham Lincoln was to be one of the speakers at the dedication of that cemetery. The keynote speaker, who preceded the President, spoke for an hour. Lincoln spoke for two minutes, saying 10 sentences, Lincoln's Gettysburg Address. Lincoln's brief remarks that day are still revered as one of the greatest American speeches ever. In the Address he paid homage to the brave heroes who had died there, but he also redefined the purpose of the war. This would now be a war to make men free. Lincoln, who had been a moderate, was now an abolitionist. For the United States, there would be no going back.

(25) Many of Mary Todd Lincoln's family in Kentucky sided with the Confederacy. Several of her brothers fought in the Confederate Army. Critics of the Lincoln administration sometimes suggested that Mary might not be in full support of the Union.

(26) By the time the election of 1864 came around, Lincoln was doubtful that he would be reelected. He had generally been an

unpopular President up to that time. By 1864 the war had lasted too long and the end was not yet in sight. Lincoln was challenged by Union General George McClellan, who was loved by his men. McClellan was in favor of discontinuing the war and allowing the South to separate. News that William Tecumseh Sherman had taken Atlanta gave Lincoln a tremendous boost just two months before the election. He ended up defeating McClellan handily.

(27) Lincoln's second inaugural address, given on March 5, 1865, with victory in sight, is one of his most famous speeches. This is the final paragraph of that speech:

> With malice toward none, with charity for all, with firmness in the right as God gives us to see the right, let us strive on to finish the work we are in, to bind up the nation's wounds, to care for him who shall have borne the battle and for his widow and his orphan, to do all which may achieve and cherish a just and lasting peace among ourselves and with all nations.[

(28) Abraham Lincoln was assassinated by an actor and Confederate sympathizer, John Wilkes Booth, on Good Friday, April 15, 1865, a week after General Robert E. Lee had surrendered the Army of Northern Virginia. Lincoln had been an unpopular President for most of his tenure; now he was a fallen hero.

(29) Abraham Lincoln is considered by most historians to have been America's greatest President.

(30) Abraham Lincoln's image is on the five dollar bill and the penny.

Quotes from Abraham Lincoln

Nearly all men can stand adversity, but if you want to test a man's character, give him power.

No man has a good enough memory to be a successful liar.

Be sure you put your feet in the right place, then stand firm.

My dream is of a place and a time where America will once again be seen as the last best hope of earth.

Character is like a tree and reputation like a shadow. The shadow is what we think of it; the tree is the real thing.

When I do good, I feel good. When I do bad, I feel bad. That's my religion.

Give me six hours to chop down a tree and I will spend the first four sharpening the axe.

Government of the people, by the people, for the people, shall not perish from the Earth.

Don't worry when you are not recognized, but strive to be worthy of recognition.

You can fool all the people some of the time, and some of the people all the time, but you cannot fool all the people all the time.

Most folks are as happy as they make up their minds to be.

Do I not destroy my enemies when I make them my friends?

I have always found that mercy bears richer fruits than strict justice.

He has a right to criticize, who has a heart to help.

Joshua Chamberlain (1828-1914), Courage and Commitment

(1) On the second day of the Battle of Gettysburg, Colonel Joshua Chamberlain's 20th Maine Regiment was assigned to defend Little Round Top, a small hill on the left flank of the Union line. Confederate forces struck Little Round Top hard, attempting to flank the Union Army. Chamberlain's men fought until they were

almost out of ammunition. Rather than surrender, Chamberlain ordered his men to fix bayonets and charge the enemy. The tactic caused panic among the Confederates, and the 20th was able to hold the flank. If Chamberlain's men had failed, the enemy would have been able to complete their flanking movement, and this could have changed the outcome of the battle and possibly the outcome of the war.

The Union victory at Gettysburg was the turning point of the war.

(2)   Joshua Chamberlain was born in Brewer, Maine. He was the oldest of five children.

(3)   Chamberlain attended Bowdoin College in Brunswick, Maine, where he became acquainted with Calvin Stowe, who was a professor at the college, and Calvin's wife, Harriet Beecher Stowe.

(4)   Joshua Chamberlain married Fanny Adams in 1855. The couple had five children, but only two of them survived into adulthood.

(5)   After graduating from Bowdoin, Chamberlain studied for three years at Bangor Theological Seminary in Bangor, Maine.

(6)   Chamberlain eventually became a professor of rhetoric at Bowdoin College. He was employed there when the Civil War began.

(7)   Chamberlain was believed to be fluent in up to ten languages.

(8)   Chamberlain volunteered for the Union Army and was appointed as a lieutenant colonel of the 20th Maine Regiment of the Army of the Potomac and saw action in the Battle of Fredericksburg.

(9)   Chamberlain was promoted to full colonel and command of his regiment in June 1863, only weeks before he would lead his men into history at the Battle of Gettysburg.

(10) Chamberlain was awarded the Medal of Honor for his courage and leadership at Gettysburg.

(11) Chamberlain was seriously wounded on June 18, 1864 at the Second Battle of Petersburg. Despite the injury, he continued to rally his men until he collapsed from loss of blood. The attending surgeon who treated him did not expect him to recover. The injury plagued him for the rest of his life.

(12) Chamberlain remained in the army for the rest of the war and was with Grant and the Army of the Potomac at Appomattox Court House. He participated in the formal ceremony of accepting the surrender of the Army of North Virginia.

(13) During his military service, Chamberlain had risen to the rank of major general.

(14) Upon returning to Maine, Chamberlain was elected to four consecutive one year terms as governor.

(15) In 1871 Joshua Chamberlain was appointed President of Bowdoin College, where he had taught before the war. He served as college president from 1871 to 1883.

Quotes from Joshua Chamberlain

The power of noble deeds is to be preserved and passed on to the future.

But the cause for which we fought was higher; our thought wider... That thought was our power.

William Tecumseh Sherman (1820-1891) and Total War

(1) General William Tecumseh Sherman played a critical role in the Union victory in the Civil War.

(2) William Tecumseh Sherman was born in Lancaster, Ohio in 1820, one of ten children. His father, a judge with the Ohio Supreme Court, died when William was nine years old. William then went to live with a family friend, Thomas Ewing Sr., a US Senator, who served as Secretary of State under Presidents Harrison and Tyler and Secretary of the Interior under President Zachary Taylor.

(3) WT Sherman attended the US Military Academy at West Point, where he proved to be an excellent student.

(4) Upon graduation from West Point, Lieutenant Sherman saw his first combat in the Second Seminole War.

(5) Unlike most other future Civil War generals, William T. Sherman had little involvement in the Mexican War. He was sent to

California after it had already been secured by John C. Fremont and Navy Commodore John D. Sloat.

(6) In 1850 William Tecumseh Sherman married his foster sister, Ellen Boyle Ewing. Her father, who was William's foster father, was the Secretary of the Interior at the time, and President Zachary Taylor attended the wedding. The Shermans would have eight children.

(7) William Tecumseh Sherman resigned from the army in 1853 and involved himself in the banking industry in San Francisco and New York City.

(8) In 1859 Sherman became the superintendent of the Louisiana State Seminary of Learning & Military Academy in Pineville, Louisiana. That school later became Louisiana State University.

(9) Sherman reentered the army to serve in the Civil War. He distinguished himself in the disastrous Battle of Bull Run, where he received minor wounds. As a result, he was promoted to brigadier general and reassigned to the western theater of war.

(10) Sherman was given command of the Union army in Kentucky, which was a difficult command. Kentucky, a border state that had remained in the Union, was highly contested with Confederate troops in control of much of the state. According to Sherman, his troops were desperately short of supplies. Sherman worried that his command had no hope. He asked to be relieved and left the army briefly with a nervous condition that he later admitted was a breakdown.

(11) At the Battle of Shiloh in April 1862, Sherman and Grant were surprised and nearly routed by Confederates under Albert Sidney Johnston on the first day of the battle. But the Union forces counterattacked on the second day and the battle ended inconclusively. Both Grant and western theater commander, Henry Halleck, praised the leadership of General Sherman, who was wounded twice during the battle.

(12) Sherman served under Grant during the siege of Vicksburg. By taking Vicksburg, the Union forces had complete control of the Mississippi River, an important factor in the eventual Union victory. But the campaign was slow moving, and the eastern

press was critical of the lack of progress. A common assertion was that the army in the west was commanded by a drunk (Grant) who was advised by a lunatic (Sherman).

(13) When Lincoln called General Grant to the east in 1864 to command the Army of the Potomac and to be overall commander of all Union troops, Grant appointed Sherman to take command of the western theater.

(14) With his new western command, General Sherman decided to direct his efforts toward Atlanta. He took the city on September 2, 1864, burning and destroying much of it. The capture of Atlanta came at a perfect time for Lincoln with the election only two months away it now appeared that the Union army was taking control of the South and the war would be won soon.

(15) From Atlanta, Sherman declined the temptation to pursue the retreating army of General Joseph Johnston. Instead he marched his army through Georgia from Atlanta to Savannah, on the coast, inflicting as much destruction as possible on the way. Sherman called this strategy "total war." The purpose was to inflict misery and break the will of the Southern society to support the war, thus bringing the war to a speedy end. The strategy did inflict misery, and it made Sherman a figure of hatred in the South, but it also saved Union lives and made Confederate leaders in the western theater more willing to surrender when the time came. In this way, Sherman may have also saved the lives of some Confederate soldiers.

(16) From Savannah, Sherman continued his march of devastation and total war through South Carolina. This first state to have seceded from the Union was punished severely by Sherman's soldiers. When Sherman's forces captured the South Carolina capital, Columbia, they again burned and destroyed much of the city. The march continued into North Carolina, but the devastation was less severe there.

(17) In 1866 after the Civil War, General Sherman was promoted to lieutenant general (3 stars), commanding western frontier armies.

(18) When Grant was elected President in 1868, General Sherman was appointed as Commanding General of the Army, the post which Grant had held before the election.

(19) General Sherman expressed racial hatred of indigenous people, and was frequently criticized for waging inhumane, total war against the Indians including the killing of women and children. He did support Indian rights on the reservation, but this is of course little consolation.

Quotes from William Tecumseh Sherman

War is cruelty. There is no use trying to reform it. The crueler it is, the sooner it will be over.

War is Hell.

Fear is the beginning of wisdom.

In our Country... one class of men makes war and leaves another to fight it out.

Ulysses Simpson Grant (1822-1885), The Relentless Pursuer

(1) Ulysses S. Grant was born and raised in southern Ohio. His name at birth was Hiram Ulysses Grant. His father ran a successful tannery.[22]

(2) US Grant's father expected his children to work in his business. Ulysses was the most reluctant because he was repulsed by the bloody carcasses.

(3) Without his knowledge and against his will, Grant's father arranged to get him an appointment into the US Military Academy at West Point.

(4) At West Point, Grant excelled at mathematics and horsemanship but did not do well in other subjects. He also grew seven inches. On entering the Academy at age 16, Grant was 5 feet 1 inch tall,

---

[22] A tannery is a facility for producing leather from the carcasses of animals.

just barely above the minimum height of 5 feet. At graduation, he was 5'8".

(5) On entering West Point, Grant adopted the name Ulysses Simpson Grant. He did not want the initials of his given name, HUG, on his equipment. The initials USG were a better fit at the US Military Academy.

(6) Grant served in the Mexican War, though he considered it to be morally wrong. Years later he wrote,

> I did not think there was ever a more wicked war than that waged by the United States on Mexico. I thought so at the time, when I was a youngster, only I had not the moral courage enough to resign.[23]

(7) During the Mexican War, Grant served first under General Zachary Taylor, where he was involved in the historic campaign that made Taylor famous. Later Grant served under Winfield Scott during his march from Vera Cruz to Mexico City, when Captain Robert E. Lee was making a name for himself.

(8) Grant resigned from the army in 1853.

(9) When the Civil War began, Grant reentered the army as a brigadier general in the western theater of war.

(10) As the war had been going badly in the east, Grant recorded the first notable success for the Union Army when he captured Fort Donelson in Tennessee in February 1862. When the Confederate commander of the fort asked Grant what would be his terms of surrender, Grant replied there were no terms only "unconditional surrender." From that time on, US Grant had the nickname "Unconditional Surrender Grant." He was also promoted to major general.

(11) Both General Grant and General Sherman were surprised by the Confederate attack at Shiloh, Tennessee, and took heavy losses

---

[23] W. E. Woodward, *Meet General Grant*, New York: Liveright, 1928, 77. Contained in William A. Degregoio, *The Complete Book of Presidents*, New York: Barricade Books, Inc., 273.

on the first day of the battle. But they counterattacked on the second day and avoided defeat.

(12) In May and June of 1863, Grant laid siege to Vicksburg, on the Mississippi River. During the long siege, the people of Vicksburg were starving and eating their horses. Vicksburg surrendered on July 4, 1863, the same day that General Lee made his retreat from Gettysburg. The Confederate army had been crippled beyond repair, and the Union was now in total control of the Mississippi River. The tide had turned decisively to the Union.

(13) In 1864 Grant was promoted to lieutenant general (3 stars) and reassign to the eastern theater to be commander of the Army of the Potomac and commanding general of the entire Union Army.

(14) During the Wilderness Campaign of 1864, Grant pursued General Lee and the Army of Northern Virginia relentlessly, while taking heavy casualties. During this campaign Grant acquired another, less complimentary nickname, "Butcher Grant." Grant's Wilderness campaign would be called a "war of attrition" today. Both sides had heavy losses. Grant's losses were much greater that those of Lee, but Grant had many more men under his command than Lee did.

(15) On April 9, 1865 at Appomattox Court House, Virginia, US Grant accepted Robert E. Lee's surrender of the Army of Northern Virginia, allowing Confederates under Lee's command generous terms. Southern armies of the west were weak and impotent by this time, so would follow suit quickly.

(16) US Grant was elected US President as a Republican in 1868 and reelected in 1872. His administration, especially during his first term, has been highly criticized for corruption. Grant, himself, was never involved in the corruption, but he appointed unscrupulous people to key positions in his cabinet. On the other hand, his administration had a solid record for its efforts to protect the rights of newly freed black Africans in the South. This was also the time of rapidly expanding industry and railroad construction in America.

(17) After leaving office Mr. and Mrs. Grant and their son, Jesse, went on an extended world tour, meeting dignitaries everywhere

they went. They met the Pope and Queen Victoria, and German Chancellor Bismarck, among many others.

(18) In 1880 the Republican Party, which had held the White House since Lincoln's election in 1860, was feeling vulnerable and looking for a popular candidate. Many party leaders proposed Grant for a third term. Grant did, in fact, lead in the first thirty-five rounds of balloting at the Republican convention that year, but in the end he did not receive the nomination.

(19) Grant opened a brokerage firm in New York City with a partner in 1884. That business went bankrupt, leaving Grant destitute.

(20) After Grant's bankruptcy, Mark Twain, who owned part of a publishing company, offered Grant a contract to write his memoirs.

(21) Grant, who was believed to have smoked 20 cigars a day, developed mouth and throat cancer shortly after he had begun to write his memoirs. He raced to complete the project in order to provide funds for his widow. He died July 23, 1885.

(22) US Grant's image is on the fifty dollar bill.

Quotes from US Grant

In every battle there comes a time when both sides consider themselves beaten, then he who continues the attack wins.

The friend in my adversity I shall always cherish most. I can better trust those who helped to relieve the gloom of my dark hours than those who are so ready to enjoy with me the sunshine of my prosperity.

If men make war in slavish obedience to rules, they will fail.

Dorothea Dix (1802-1887), Nursing the Wounded

(1) During the Civil War, Dorothea Dix was appointed Director of Nursing for the Union Army. She made regulations for the nurses to protect them from abuse and harassment. But what she became most known for at that time was her insistence that Confederate prisoners be cared for with the same treatment as Union casualties.

(2) Dorothea Dix was born in Maine and raised in Massachusetts. She was the daughter of a Protestant preacher, who may also have been an alcoholic.

(3) Fleeing an unhappy childhood, Dorothea came to live with her grandmother in Boston at age 12.

(4) In 1821 Dorothea opened a school in Boston, but also taught indigent children out of her grandmother's barn.

(5) Dorothea Dix authored several books, which tended to focus on personal growth.

(6) Dix suffered from poor health and depression much of her life.

(7) From 1831 until 1836, Dix operated a school for girls in Boston.

(8) While visiting England around 1840, Dorothea Dix became interested in reform of mental health facilities.

(9) Dix took it upon herself to do an extensive study of the treatment of the mentally ill in Massachusetts. She was shocked and upset. She submitted a detailed report to the Massachusetts legislature.

(10) In 1844, Ms. Dix made another extensive investigation of mental health facilities, this one in New Jersey. She also included jails and poorhouses in this survey. And she again compiled a detailed report. This was submitted to the New Jersey legislature.

(11) Dix traveled through many states after 1844, investigating mental health facilities, jails, and poorhouses, compiling and submitting detailed reports to state legislatures.

(12) Many states instituted reforms after considering the reports of Dorothea Dix.

(13) In 1854-1855 Dix visited Europe again. At that time she investigated the mental health facilities in Scotland. Her report

led directly to the formation of The Scottish Lunacy Commission to oversee reforms.

(14) Dix continued and expanded her investigations in Europe and parts of Canada. She was granted a meeting with the Pope in Rome, and convince him to investigate facilities in that city, which he found to be shocking.

(15) After the Civil War, Dix resumed her life's work investigating mental health facilities, concentering on the conditions in the South, as the war had degraded much of that region.

Quotes from Dorothea Dix

Your minds may now be likened to a garden, which will, if neglected, yield only weeds and thistles; but, if cultivated, will produce the most beautiful flowers, and the most delicious fruits.

What greater bliss than to look back on days spent in usefulness, in doing good to those around us.

I have had so much at heart. Defeated, not conquered; disappointed, not discouraged. I have but to be more energetic and more faithful in the difficult and painful vocation to which my life is devoted.

With care and patience, people may accomplish things which, to an indolent[24] person, would appear impossible.

The duties of a teacher are neither few nor small, but they elevate the mind and give energy to the character.

My wish is to be known only thru my work.

---

[24] Indolent: lazy

PART 2

THE POST-CIVIL WAR
THROUGH WORLD WAR I

The US Civil War, which ended in April 1865, created two profound changes in America: (1) the emancipation of millions of former slaves in the southern US; and (2) the impetus toward rapid industrialization and economic expansion.[25]

Evolutionary changes were also at work in late nineteenth century America. Indigenous tribes in the west which had benefited from the distraction of the Civil War, were now confronted with a more aggressive encroachment, and the movement for equal rights for women, more specifically the right to vote, which had been gaining momentum when the Civil War broke out, was continuing. Women were not allowed to vote in most states until the passage of the 19th amendment in 1920.[26]

---

[25] Emancipation: The 13th Amendment to the US Constitution made slavery illegal, thus freeing (emancipating) the slaves.

Impetus: That which encourages or moves a process forward.

[26] Amendment: To amend is to change. A constitutional amendment is a change or an addition made to the constitution after its adoption. In the US Constitution amendments are rare because they required a vote of approval in ¾ of the states and 2/3 of both Houses of Congress.

CHAPTER 7

THE RISE OF AFRICAN-AMERICANS, 1865-1914

To fully grasp the achievements of African-American culture in the time between the Civil War and World War I (1865-1914), we must first understand the forces working against African-Americans. There were many.

(1)   Slaves had been systematically denied education. In the slave states, it had been a crime to teach a slave to read and write, and slaves who attempted to teach themselves were punished for their effort if they were detected.

(2)   Most former slaves had little experience or training with property ownership or handling personal and family finances.

(3)   Many white people considered dark skinned people inferior and expected them to fail. This erroneous belief in the superiority of the white race was common even among educated people in the nineteenth century.[27] The famous 1889 poem "The White Man's Burden" by English poet Rudyard Kipling illustrates the beliefs of the time well.

(4)   There were few laws to support equality, and many laws in the South supported segregation.[28]

(5)   Employment discrimination was normal and legal at the time. In general this meant that African-Americans were the last hired and the first fired. They were also denied many clean, well-paying jobs and often had to settle for jobs which no one else wanted and which paid less.

---

[27] Erroneous: false; in error; mistaken.
[28] Segregation: the enforced separation of races.

(6) The economy of the former Confederacy had been destroyed in the Civil War.[29] There was much physical destruction, the greatest example of which was that inflicted by (General) Sherman's famous March to the Sea by which the army under William T. Sherman marched unopposed from Atlanta to Savannah in Georgia, cutting a wide path and destroying everything in it. There was also the loss from the cost of war materials and resources invested in the war. There were losses from the effects of the successful union blockade during the war.[30] Many southerners were reduced to abject poverty and near starvation by the war. Then there was of course the direct loss of the asset of slave labor for which many plantation owners had paid a great amount of money. The southern states, where most former slaves lived, continued to be impoverished well into the twentieth century.

(7) African-Americans were scapegoats for white southern frustration.[31] They were looked upon by many as the cause of their poverty. They were also seen as an economic threat, as they began to compete with poor whites. Early twentieth century race riots in Atlanta and East Saint Louis in which whites attacked blacks appear to have been caused primarily by competition for jobs.

(8) The white governing classes of the South tried to reestablish the old social order despite emancipation. African-Americans were commonly harassed, threatened, and assaulted by whites, especially in the South. Lynching of African-Americans was epidemic in the South.[32] A system of agriculture known as

---

[29] Confederacy (officially known as the Confederate States of America): These were the 11 southern states which attempted to secede (withdraw) from the United States after the election of Abraham Lincoln as President in 1860.

[30] Blockade: A naval action which prevents goods from entering or leaving a country as a tactic of war.

[31] Scapegoat: A person or thing blamed for a situation for which that person or thing had no real involvement.

[32] Lynching: hanging a person by the neck to kill that person without the process of law.

Epidemic: the rapid spread of a disease or social phenomenon.

"share-cropping" developed by which the impoverished "share-cropper" farmed, but did not own, the land. The land owner purchased the seeds and tools for planting. At harvest, a share of the crop was paid to the land owner and a share was kept by the tenant after the tenant had repaid the owner for seeds and other expenses. The effect of the system was to keep the tenant in perpetual debt to the land owner, and state laws often forbade a tenant who owed money to the land owner from quitting. So this became a slightly more evolved and subtle form of slavery. Victims of the system included poor whites as well as African-Americans.

The African-American Response

The rise of African-Americans in the years immediately after the Civil War is an amazing story of determination, dignity, and grace exhibited by millions of Americans. This is a story of a slow, incremental struggle with incomplete success. Our brief look into this phenomenon during the years 1865 to 1914 will be concentrated on three principal leaders: Booker T. Washington, Ida B. Wells, and W.E.B. DuBois. Washington became a great educator. His message was *lift yourself up*. Ida Wells set a standard for investigative journalism, while standing up with courage. And W.E.B. Du Bois demanded full equality while debunking the myth of white superiority by earning a Ph.D. at Harvard and becoming a renowned professor at that school. The African-American struggle for full equality lasted well into the 1970s and beyond. Many African-Americans contend that this struggle continues today.

Booker T. Washington (1856-1915) and Tuskegee Institute

(1) Booker T. Washington was born a slave in Virginia in 1856. His father was a white man who was not involved in Booker's life. Through his own effort, Booker gained an education and rose to become the director of a legendary educational institution, the

unofficial spokesman for African-Americans, and an advisor to US presidents.

(2) When Booker T. Washington arrived in Hampton, Virginia, hoping to be admitted to Hampton Institute to begin a serious education, he had no money and had slept outside for several days during his journey.

(3) Washington was allowed to work his way through Hampton Institute as a janitor.

(4) At age 25 recent Hampton graduate, Booker T. Washington, was named to be the first principal of the newly established Tuskegee Normal School (teachers' school). The school name was soon changed to Tuskegee Institute.

(5) Tuskegee Institute, which Washington led, was a teachers' college which also emphasized development of practical skills. Faced with grossly unfair social conditions which included violent suppression of blacks, Washington philosophized that no one can control the actions of others, but everyone can improve his/her own life through personal effort and, in the long-run, people will respect proven ability and genuine accomplishment.

(6) Under BT Washington, Tuskegee Institute engaged in various commercial enterprises in order to be self-sustaining. One of these enterprises was the manufacture of bricks for construction. But no one at Tuskegee knew much about the process in the beginning. As a result Tuskegee (and Washington) failed three times at great expense before they got the process right. Once the process was established, Tuskegee student labor was used to construct new buildings as the school grew. In this way, the students also learned useful construction skills. Tuskegee also became the leading supplier of bricks for all construction projects in a wide region which included several southern states.

(7) In 1896 BT Washington was able to recruit botanist George Washington Carver to Tuskegee Institute. Carver chaired the Agricultural Department at Tuskegee for 47 years and made significant advances in agriculture, especially those involving peanuts, notably the development of peanut butter.[33]

---

[33] Botanist: a scientist who studies plants.

(8)   Booker T. Washington gave a famous speech at the Atlanta Exposition of 1895. It this speech, he proposed what became known as "the Atlanta Compromise." His suggestion was that African-Americans would obey the laws and not protest, while white Americans would allow them basic human rights and access to education, and the entire society could remain socially segregated.

He believed that if African-Americans proved themselves worthy through hard work, they would eventually be accepted as equals. This made sense and seemed possible to many African-Americans in 1895 with the Civil War only 30 years past, though white society in the South hateful toward African-Americans.

(9)   Booker T. Washington became the first black man to eat dinner with the US President (Theodore Roosevelt) in the White House. This might seem unremarkable now, but at that time it was major news and caused some white resentment.

(10) BT Washington's autobiography, *Up from Slavery*, has inspired many young people—black and white.

Quotes from B.T. Washington

Nothing ever comes to one that is worth having, except as a result of hard work.

Success is to be measured not so much by the position that one has reached in life as by the obstacles which he has overcome.

If you want to lift yourself up, lift up someone else.

Excellence is to do a common thing in an uncommon way.

Associate yourself with people of good quality, for it is better to be alone than in bad company.

I shall allow no man to belittle my soul by making me hate him.

There are two ways of exerting one's strength: one is pushing down, the other is pulling up.

Character, not circumstances, makes the man (or a woman).

One man cannot hold another man down in the ditch without remaining down in the ditch with him.

The individual who can do something that the world wants done will, in the end, make his way regardless of his race.

Dignify and glorify common labor. It is at the bottom of life that we must begin, not at the top.

Ida B. Wells (1862-1931), the First Investigative Journalist

(1) Ida B. Wells was born into slavery in Mississippi during the Civil War. After the war her parents became strong advocates for education and impressed the importance of education on Ida. She would became a groundbreaking journalist.

(2) Ida's primary education was by white teachers who were sent by the Freedmen's Bureau into the south after the Civil War to help African-Americans learn to read and write.

(3) Ida was orphaned at age 16 when her parents and one brother died in a yellow fever epidemic.

(4) Wells began her career as a teacher in Memphis, Tennessee. She taught there for five years. Her teaching career ended when she was fired for openly criticizing the conditions and lack of funding for Africa-American schools. (Most schools in America were segregated at that time.)

(5) Wells is most famous as an investigative journalist during a time when investigative journalism was almost un-thought of. Her primary focus was a detailed study of the lynchings of African-Americans in the south in the 1890s. Her most famous work is *The Red Record*, a three year study completed in 1895.

(6) Wells was involved with many social issues. She tried to establish a settlement house in Chicago for African-Americans migrating from the south. This was modeled after the famous Hull House founded by Jane Addams. The Wells version was short lived because Wells was unable to find sufficient donor money. Wells was also involved in the women's voting rights movement.

(7) Ida Wells published her autobiography, *A Divided Duty*, in which she wrote about her struggle to balance home life and child rearing with her career as a journalist and activist.

Quotes from Ida B. Wells

Somebody must show that the Afro-American race is more sinned against than sinning, and it seems to have fallen upon me to do so.

The people must know before they can act, and there is no educator to compare with the press.

W. E. B. DuBois (1868-1963) and the NAACP

(1) W.E.B. DuBois was born in Massachusetts in 1868. His father had served in the Union Army during the Civil War.

(2) W.E.B. DuBois was the first African-American to earn a doctorate (Ph.D.) degree at Harvard.

(3) DuBois became a rival of Booker T. Washington. The cause of their conflict was in their approaches as to how best to elevate African-Americans to equality. Washington saw the solution in the educational development of African-Americans to increased levels of competence for all with emphasis on practical skills. His "Atlanta Compromise" solution also included the temporary acceptance of an inferior social status for African-Americans. DuBois, on the other hand, believed that African-Americans needed to be assertive and demand their rights. The difference might be in that BT Washington was a man of the nineteenth century, while Du Bois was of the twentieth century.

(4) DuBois was an organizer of the Niagara Movement, begun with a meeting at Niagara Falls in 1905. Participants renounced BT Washington's accommodation approach in favor of stronger demands for equal treatment.

(5) While BT Washington wanted to improve the skills and status of the poorest African-Americans, DuBois emphasized development for "the talented tenth" (the brightest) African-Americans while being highly critical of lower classes as lazy. In hindsight we might say that both men had some good ideas which advanced the American society, but maybe neither had a complete solution.

(6) DuBois was involved with the Pan-African movement of the early twentieth century. The purpose of the movement was to encourage the decolonization of Africa and African self-government.

(7) DuBois was among the founders of the National Association for the Advancement of Colored People (NAACP). He insisted on the use of the word "colored" in the official title because he envisioned the organization as opposing discrimination against many racial/ethnic groups, not just black people.

(8) DuBois published many books, the most famous of which is *The Souls of Black Folk*.

(9) W.E.B. DuBois lived 95 years. During most of those years he struggled for equality in America. Near the end of his life he left the US and renounced his US citizenship. He died days before Martin Luther King's famous "Dream Speech."

Quotes from W.E.B. DuBois

A little less complaint and whining, and a little more dogged work and manly striving, would do us more credit than a thousand civil rights bills.

The cost of liberty is less than the price of repression.

A Final Word

While it is right to applaud African-American resistance to racial inequality, and it is true that many white Americans saw the injustice and did nothing; it is naive and unfair to paint the problem in the United States as strictly one of white suppression and black resistance.[34] Some white people were notably involved in trying to solve the problem. Prominent white Americans involved in the advancement of the African-American cause between 1865 and 1914 include the following.

Thaddeus Stephens was the leading outspoken defender of African-American rights in the US Congress in the years immediately following the Civil War.

Civil War General **O. O. Howard**, for whom the traditionally African-American Howard University is named, was the head of the Freedman's Bureau after the war, attempting to uplift African-Americans through education.

Another former Civil War general, **Samuel C. Armstrong**, was the long-time head of Hampton Institute, the school where Booker T. Washington was educated. In his autobiography, *Up from Slavery*, Washington said of Armstrong that he was "the noblest, and rarest of human beings that it has ever been my privilege to meet."[35]

In the end the struggle for equality was one for African-Americans to win. Whites could only provide limited assistance. And though great efforts had been made, the struggle was far from won in 1914. The real struggle which would propel the United States forward was not to come until the 1950s and 1960s.

---

[34] Naïve: unsophisticated, gullible, simple minded.
[35] Booker T. Washington, *Up from Slavery*, Penguin Classics, 1986 edition, p. 54.

CHAPTER 8

RESISTANCE AND STRUGGLE OF INDIGENOUS AMERICANS IN THE WEST, 1864-1890

From the period immediately after the Civil War until near the end of the nineteenth century, brave Americans fought valiantly for their land and their dignity in the face of a Goliath.[36] The Goliath was the US government, more specifically the US Army. Within the confines of this single chapter, we will examine only a few major events. For those who would like a more detailed account of the Indian conflicts in the west, two excellent books have already been written. *Bury My Heart at Wounded Knee* by Dee Brown, 1970, is a comprehensive account of most of the major conflicts. *A Century of Dishonor* by Helen Hunt Jackson, 1881, awakened European-Americans, causing them angst,[37] and leading to efforts to reform US policy toward indigenous people. Unfortunately, lack of understanding of the mindset of indigenous people meant that well-meaning reform efforts sometimes helped no one and were sometimes counterproductive to their goal of justice for Indians.

Major events in the West between 1864 and 1890 are these:

(1)   The **Sand Creek Massacre** in Colorado Territory in 1864. Cheyenne and Arapaho tribes had signed and adhered to the Treaty of Fort Laramie in 1851. The treaty held until the discovery of gold in the Rocky Mountains in 1858 and the subsequent Pikes Peak Gold Rush. Conflicts which arose, caused the federal

---

[36] Goliath: the giant killed by David in the Bible story.
[37] Angst: a feeling of unhappiness, often with a vague feeling of guilt.

government to renegotiate the treaty in 1861, greatly reducing the size of the reservations. The indigenous community split with the minority accepting the new treaty. Those who did not accept the treaty, simply ignored it, continuing to hunt on their traditional land. Those hunting outside the newly established reservations were attacked by the Colorado militia. This began a war, which was not supported by all the Indians.

Peaceful Southern Cheyenne and a few Arapaho, led by Black Kettle, were told by the Colorado governor to go to Sand Creek and fly the American flag as a sign of peace, and that they would be safe there. Despite the guarantee, the encampment, consisting of mostly women, children, and old men, was fallen upon by the Colorado militia under John Chivington. Everyone (somewhere around 100 to 150 people) was killed, and the bodies were mutilated. The later hostility of Cheyenne and Arapaho is understandable.

(2) **Red Cloud's War**, 1866-1868. Red Cloud's War is notable because it featured the second biggest battle victory by indigenous fighters against the US Army in the west and a rare victorious war of indigenous people. When the US established the Bozeman Trail to the gold fields of Montana, Lakota Sioux, Cheyenne, and Arapaho resisted with regular raids along the trail. By the 1851 Treaty of Fort Laramie, the land containing the Bozeman Trail belonged to the Crow, and they sided with the United States against their traditional enemies.

On one rare occasion in December 1866 when a large band of Sioux, Cheyenne, and Arapaho confronted the US Army, the entire command of Captain William Fetterman, 81 men, was wiped out. At the time this was the worst defeat of US army forces by indigenous forces west of the Mississippi River. The bodies of the dead soldiers were mutilated.

The 1868 Treaty of Fort Laramie ended the war, assigning the disputed land around the Bozeman Trail to the Lakota. The forts along the trail were dismantled and the trail was permanently closed.

(3)   **The Great Sioux War** and **Custer's Last Stand**, 1876. The terms of the 1868 treaty, which had ended Red Cloud's War, were violated when gold was discovered in the Black Hills on Lakota Sioux land. In this 1876 war, the Sioux were again allied with the Cheyenne and the Arapaho. The most notable event of the war was the defeat of the Seventh US Cavalry under General George Armstrong Custer in the Battle of the Little Bighorn River. Custer had been overly confident, choosing to split his forces. Those 200 plus men remaining under Custer's direct command were attacked by a force of approximately 3000 Sioux, Cheyenne, and Arapaho. All the US soldiers and their commander were killed. This was the greatest single defeat of the US army by indigenous Americans west of the Mississippi River. News of the defeat reached the east as the nation was celebrating the July 4 centennial of the United States (1876).

(4)   **The Retreat of the Nez Perce**, 1877. The Nez Perce had never made war on the United States. They signed and adhered to the 1855 Treaty of Walla Walla. In violation of that treaty, the Nez Perce were ordered to a reservation in Idaho. Some Nez Perce complied; many did not. Those who refused the new reservation fled east with the US army in pursuit. Unable to gain allies to the east, the Nez Perce (and a few Palouse) decided to try to join Sitting Bull, the Sioux chief who had fled to Canada. The Nez Perce continued to flee to the east while attempting to turn north with most of the US Army in the west after them. With skirmishes along the way, the Nez Perce covered a distance of more than 1,000 miles with their families over five months. They were finally captured near the Canadian border when they encamped without posting guards, possibly thinking that they had crossed into Canada. Even in the final siege, surrounded by the US Army, the Nez Perce held out for five days before surrendering.

(5)   **The Wounded Knee Massacre**, 1890. The Lakota Sioux had continued to suffer from encroachment[38] onto their land. The buffalo herds had been all but completely wiped out. A Paiute

---

[38] Encroachment: trespassing or intrusion.

prophet, Wovoka, was teaching among the Sioux and leading "Ghost Dance" ceremonies which he said would bring back dead ancestors and restore prosperity. The Ghost Dance began to draw large crowds, and the US army began to see it as a threat.

On the day of the massacre, December 29. 1890, 350 Sioux (230 men and 120 women and children) were encamped at Wounded Knee Creek under guard by 500 soldiers of the Seventh Cavalry, Custer's former command. On that day, the soldiers ordered the Sioux to disarm, and the soldiers searched the camp. A few of the Sioux men were able to hide their weapons under their blankets on this cold winter day. When one of these men was discovered to be in possession of his weapon a scuffle developed. Others Sioux pulled out their weapons and a battle began. With only a few Sioux armed, the US army soldiers began to fire indiscriminately, killing unarmed people including women and children. At least 150 Sioux were killed and 51 Sioux wounded, 39 US soldiers were killed and more than 220 wounded. The recently developed Hotchkiss gun, an early type of rapid fire weapon, inflicted many of the Sioux casualties, and many of the US casualties were from stray Hotchkiss bullets. A court of inquiry was ordered, but all US forces were exonerated. More than twenty US soldiers were awarded the Medal of Honor for their involvement in the incident. This was the last major clash of the Indian Wars.

Red Cloud and the Bozeman Trail, 1822-1909

(1)   Red Cloud, a chief of the Oglala Sioux, led a successful war against the US Army from 1866 to 1868. The cause of that war had been heavy European-American use of the Bozeman Trail going to the gold fields of Montana through traditional Indian land.

(2)   Early enemies of the Sioux were the Pawnee and the Crow.

(3)   Red Cloud's War pitted Sioux, Cheyenne, and Arapaho against the US army and the Crow.

(4) Red Cloud's biggest victory was the massacre of Captain William J. Fedderman's command in December 1866. Fedderman had been baited into a trap by Crazy Horse. When the trap was sprung, 2000 indigenous fighters wiped out Fedderman's force of 81.

(5) Red Cloud's War ended with the Bozeman Trail permanently closed.

(6) Red Cloud went to Washington, DC in 1875 to plead with President Grant to enforce the treaty of 1868 and prevent European-Americans from invading Sioux land after gold had been discovered in the Black Hills of the Sioux Reservation the previous year.

(7) During his trip to Washington, Red Cloud became convinced that war against the United States would be futile. When war did break out in1876, Red Cloud and his band did not participate.

(8) Red Cloud converted to Catholicism and was baptized in 1884.

(9) Red Cloud protested the Dawes Act of 1887 which split up communally held reservation land into individual tracks. By that law each head of household was granted 160 acres of land with any excess to be sold off.

(10) Red Cloud lived until 1909, so he saw the last of all the Indian Wars and the beginnings of stable reservation life. He became the most photographed indigenous leader of the nineteenth century. He died at age 87.

Quotes from Red Cloud

We do not want riches but we do want to train our children right. Riches would do us no good. We could not take them with us to the other world. We do not want riches. We want peace and love.

In a war with other nations, I was in eighty-seven fights. There I received my name and was made Chief of my nation. But now I am old and am for peace.

Even if you live forty or fifty years in this world, and then die, you cannot take all your goods with you.

Sitting Bull (c. 1831-1890) and Custer's Last Stand

(1) In 1864 Sitting Bull saw his first combat against the US Army. During one skirmish, he was shot through the hip with the bullet existing in the small of his back.

(2) Sitting Bull participated in Red Cloud's War of 1866-1868, then refused to accept the treaty ending that war. He continued to raid the US Army and European-American travelers for the next several years, while living on and off the reservation and hunting wherever he felt the need to.

(3) When the Northern Pacific Railroad was attempting to establish a route through the Dakotas in the early 1870s, surveying parties were attacked and harassed by Sitting Bull's band.

(4) After gold was discovered in the Black Hills in 1874 and large numbers of European-Americans flooded into the area, Sitting Bull led more frequent raids.

(5) Sitting Bull participation in the Great Sioux War of 1876-1877. He, together with Crazy Horse, led the Sioux, Cheyenne, and Arapaho forces in the Battle of the Little Bighorn, the greatest indigenous victory since the 1791 Battle of the Wabash.

(6) When faced with the overwhelming force of the US Army in 1877, as other war leaders surrendered, Sitting Bull led his band north into Canada, where they remained for four years.

(7) While in Canada, Sitting Bull established peaceful relations with the Canadian government and the Blackfeet, a traditional enemy of the Sioux.

(8) The difficulties of finding food in the frigid north caused Sitting Bull to lead his band of 200 back into the United States and surrender in 1881.

(9) In 1884 and 1885 Sitting Bull appeared in "Wild West" shows. He became very fond of Annie Oakley and friends with Buffalo Bill Cody.

(10) Through his Wild West show appearances, Sitting Bull became famous throughout the US. He capitalized on this by selling photographs of himself and did well with this endeavor.

(11) During the 1890 Ghost Dance phenomena on the Sioux reservation, US officials feared that Sitting Bull would join the Ghost Dance movement and encourage another Indian War. Indian agency police, Sioux tribal members, were sent to arrest him. He resisted and a scuffle broke out between the police and a few Sitting Bull supporters. In that scuffle, Sitting Bull was shot in the head by a police officer.

Quotes from Sitting Bull

If we must die, we die defending our rights.

Each man is good in His sight. It is not necessary for eagles to be crows.

Let us put our minds together and see what life we can make for our children.

The white man knows how to make everything, but he does not know how to distribute it.

It is through this mysterious power that we too have our being, and we therefore yield to our neighbors, even to our animal neighbors, the same right as ourselves to inhabit this vast land.

Chief Joseph (1840-1904) and the Retreat of the Nez Perce

(1) Joseph's father was a chief of the same band of the Nez Perce tribe of which Joseph, himself, would later become chief.

(2) The Nez Perce reservation was established by the Treaty of Walla Walla in 1855 of which Joseph's father was one of the signers.

(3) A gold rush in 1863 resulted in the US government renegotiating the 1855 treaty. This caused a split among the Nez Perce with some bands accepting the new treaty and relocating to a smaller reservation. Joseph's band refused the new treaty, stayed on their land, resisted encroachment, and tried to resist the use of violence.

(4) In 1873 Joseph came to an agreement with the federal government, which allowed his band to stay on their land.

(5) By 1877 the US government had again unilaterally decided to move the Nez Perce. Joseph at first reluctantly began to prepare for the journey. A skirmish between Nez Perce and some European-Americans resulted in the deaths of four of the whites. Nez Perce refusal to turn over the tribal members involved precipitated the legendary chase.

(6) Chief Joseph does not appear to have been in over-all command of the Nez Perce during the retreat, but rather one of a council of chiefs. After several of the other chiefs had been killed, Joseph was left as senior chief when his forces were surrounded and hopelessly outmanned. Joseph surrendered saying, "I will fight no more forever."

(7) In 1879 Joseph visited Washington, DC for the first time. He met with President Rutherford B. Hayes to plea for the reestablishment of his original reservation.

(8) In 1897 on his second trip the Washington, DC, Chief Joseph rode with Buffalo Bill in a parade honoring the memory of US Grant.

Quotes from Chief Joseph

It makes my heart sick when I remember all the good words and the broken promises.

The earth is the mother of all people, and all people should have equal rights upon it.

All men were made by the Great Spirit Chief. They are all brothers.

I believe much trouble would be saved if we opened our hearts more.

I would give up everything rather than have the blood of white men upon the hands of my people.

I hope that no more groans of wounded men and women will ever go to the ear of the Great Spirit Chief above, and that all people may be one people.

A man who would not love his father's grave is worse than a wild animal.

CHAPTER 9

AMERICAN INVENTION, DEVELOPMENT, AND ENTREPRENEURSHIP, 1865-1914

The post-Civil War years saw the rapid expansion of the US economy fueled by capital (investment money) acquired during the war, excess capacity (of former war suppliers), and innovations such as the telephone, the light bulb, and the use of the assembly line. The continued rapid expansion of the railroad also created a demand for steel which led to innovations in steel production. By the early twentieth century, the US was the leading industrial producer in the world.

Andrew Carnegie (1835-1919), Man of Steel

(1) Andrew Carnegie was born in Scotland. He immigrated to the United States with his parents in 1848.

(2) Carnegie was self-educated. He did not have time for school. At the age of 13 he was working 12 hours a day, 6 days a week to help support his family.

(3) In 1849 Carnegie got a job as a telegraph messenger boy and used that position to start acquainting himself with important people in the railroad industry. He also benefited from the friendship of an employer who allowed Carnegie to borrow books from his personal library, of which young Andrew took full advantage in educating himself.

(4) Carnegie soon moved into the railroad industry and worked his way up to Superintendent of the Western Division of the Pennsylvania Railroad.

(5) By investing in the railroad industry, Carnegie began to build his wealth.

(6) During the Civil War, Andrew Carnegie was appointed Superintendent for the Military Railways and the Union Government's telegraph lines in the East.

(7) Shrewd and lucky investments allowed Carnegie's wealth to grow. Carnegie Steel eventually became his main focus.

(8) The organization which Carnegie developed is described as vertically integrated. The goal was to control a systems of steel production and use from mining through final production of steel goods.

(9) Carnegie Steel introduced the Bessemer process of steel manufacture to America.

(10) Carnegie had a negative side. His factory employees complained of low pay and dangerous working conditions.

(11) After selling Carnegie Steel, Andrew Carnegie was the richest man in America.

(12) Andrew Carnegie is famous as a philanthropist. He gave away most of his fortune. He called for other wealthy people to do the same, following what he called "the Gospel of Wealth."

(13) Carnegie gave generously to the New York City Public Library, and he established Carnegie-Mellon University in Pittsburg and Carnegie Hall in NYC. These are his best known projects today.

Quotes from Andrew Carnegie

As I grow older, I pay less attention to what men say. I just watch what they do.

No man will make a great leader who wants to do it all himself or get all the credit for doing it.

People who are unable to motivate themselves must be content with mediocrity, no matter how impressive their other talents.

All honor's wounds are self-inflicted.

Surplus wealth is a sacred trust which its possessor is bound to administer in his lifetime for the good of the community.

Alexander Graham Bell (1847-1922), Inventor of the Telephone

(1) Alexander Graham Bell, like Andrew Carnegie, was born in Scotland.
(2) Unlike Andrew Carnegie, Alexander Graham Bell came from a middle class family. His father was a university professor.
(3) Bell migrated with his family to Canada around 1870. From there he came to study in Boston.
(4) Bell's interest in sound and sound amplification stemmed from the fact that both his mother and his wife were deaf.
(5) Bell opened a school for the deaf in Boston in 1872.
(6) Bell is famous for his 1876 invention of the telephone.
(7) Bell was a founding member of the National Geographic Society.

Quotes from Alexander Graham Bell

Sometimes we stare so long at a door that is closing that we see too late the one that is open.

Before anything else, preparation is the key to success.

A man, as a general rule, owes very little to what he is born with - a man is what he makes of himself.

Thomas Edison (1847-1931), the Wizard of Menlo Park

(1)   Thomas Edison was home schooled by his mother after a teacher had asserted that young Thomas could not be taught because he was not intelligent enough. Thomas was devoted to his mother and stated that he never wanted to disappoint her.

(2)   Thomas Edison began as a telegraph operator for the railroad. His first patents are devices involving the telegraph. The stock "ticker tape" system is an early Edison invention. Edison was eventually fired from his railroad job because he conducted experiments while working and caused some damage to train cars.

(3)   Edison, the great inventor, registered 1093 US patents. His most famous inventions were the phonograph, the motion picture camera, and the light bulb.

(4)   Edison established what is believed to have been the world's first industrial research and development laboratory in Menlo Park, New Jersey, employing a team of scientists, inventors, and engineers. He is often referred to as "the Wizard of Menlo Park." He is revered as one of the greatest inventors of all time.

(5)   Edison founded 14 companies. The largest and most famous of these, General Electric, still exists today.

(6)   While working on the light bulb, Edison said that he had not failed, he had found 100 ways not to make a light bulb.

Quotes from Thomas Edison

Our greatest weakness lies in giving up. The most certain way to succeed is always to try just one more time.

Genius is one percent inspiration and ninety-nine percent perspiration.

Nearly every man who develops an idea works it up to the point where it looks impossible, and then he gets discouraged. That's not the place to become discouraged.

Henry Ford (1863-1947) and the Great American Automobile

(1) Henry Ford studied engineering in college.

(2) Ford did not invent the automobile, nor did he invent the assembly line. But he used the assembly line technique to produce the first affordable automobiles for the mass market.

(3) The Ford manufacturing system involved producing an affordable automobile while paying relatively high wages. Ford's famous "$5 per day" was nearly double the going wage for unskilled labor at that time. Ford was willing to pay the higher wage in order to retain workers, reasoning that the cost of constantly training new workers would be more expensive in the long-run. One probably unexpected benefit was that soon Ford workers were able to purchase Ford cars themselves, thus greatly expanding the market for automobiles.

(4) Ford's first auto manufacturing company failed.

(5) Ford's genius was as an industrialist. He was not an enlightened social thinker.[39] He was, for example, famously anti-Semitic.[40]

Quotes from Henry Ford

Coming together is a beginning; keeping together is progress; working together is success.

If you think you can do a thing or think you can't do a thing, you're right.

Most people spend more time and energy going around problems than trying to solve them.

---

[39] Enlightened: free-thinking, open-minded, tolerant. (Henry Ford was NOT socially enlightened.)

[40] Anti-Semitic: This term is commonly used as an adjective to describe someone who has a prejudice against Jewish people.

CHAPTER 10

THE STRUGGLE FOR WOMEN'S RIGHTS, 1848-1920

The status of women in the United States in the early 19th century was roughly the same as the status of other women around the world. The woman was treated almost as a possession of man. The situation is best illustrated by the custom of land ownership and inheritance. Typically land was held in the husband's name. When a husband died, the land would pass to a son or sons. It would not be inherited by the widow. The son then had the right to evict his mother if he so chose.

Women generally did not work outside the home until the late 19th century, though they often shared the work on a farm. Exceptions were rare; one was the manufacturing town of Lowell, Massachusetts. The textile factory at Lowell employed young, single women to sew garments. The women in Lowell lived in a company boarding house under supervision. There was usually a 10 o'clock curfew, men were not allowed into the house, and trips out of town were discouraged. Most of the women worked up to 70 hours per week for half the standard wage of a man. When a woman married she was expected to quit working outside the home. In the case of divorce the custody of the children normally went to the father.

A national women's convention met in Seneca Falls New York in 1848 to plan ways of resisting the unfair practices of the time. The concept of such a meeting was revolutionary, but the delegates had no idea at the beginning how revolutionary this meeting would be. The convention organizer and president, Elizabeth Cady Stanton, a respectable, New York family woman, proposed the unthinkable (at that time)—that women should have the right to vote. Mrs. Stanton was able to persuade the majority of the women at the convention to vote in favor of the proposal, even though many believed that this demand went too far.

Stanton continued the push for the right to vote for the rest of her life. The demand picked up support throughout the rest of the 19th century. A key proponent for the cause, Susan B. Anthony, joined the movement in the 1850's. Stanton and Anthony became partners in the leadership of the women's right to vote movement. An interesting duo they were too. Stanton was short and stout. She was married and would have a total of 7 children. Anthony was tall and slender. She remained single her entire life stating that she would not be owned by any man.

Of course, the struggle for women's rights involved issues other than just voting. Voting was just a method of achieving equality and liberty. Access to education and careers for women was unfairly limited. Elizabeth Blackwell broke through a previously impenetrable barrier to become America's first female medical doctor in 1849. And Margaret Sanger defended the rights of women to chart their own destiny by controlling reproduction.

Elizabeth Cady Stanton (1815-1902) and the Seneca Falls Revolution

(1) Elizabeth Cady Stanton was the main organizer and president of the Seneca Falls Women's Conference of 1848. She wrote the *Declaration of Sentiments* which was adopted as the main statement of the conference. In it she demanded that women be allowed the right to vote.

(2) Elizabeth Cady was born in New York in 1815. Her father was a lawyer and politician who would eventually become a member of the New York Supreme Court.

(3) Elizabeth Cady attended a coeducational academy until the age of 16. This was highly unusual for girls at that time. Most girls were educated at home. Those who did attend school usually attended female academies. Stanton received her higher education at Troy

Female Seminary in Troy, New York (the best option available for a young lady at that time).

(4) In 1840 Elizabeth Cady married Henry Stanton, an abolitionist journalist who later became a lawyer.

(5) Elizabeth insisted that the word "obey" be omitted from the marriage vow at her wedding.

(6) Stanton supported the movement to abolish slavery, but she and Susan B. Anthony both opposed the constitutional amendment which gave black men the right to vote, because the amendment did not include the right of women to vote.

(7) Elizabeth Cady Stanton first joined forces with Susan B. Anthony around 1851 when both were active in the temperance movement in New York.[41]

(8) Stanton was a talented speech writer, but family duties often limited her travel. Consequently, she wrote many speeches that were delivered by Susan B. Anthony during their 50 year association.

(9) Stanton's support for women's rights continued to extend beyond just voting rights to include such issues as gender-neutral divorce laws, a woman's right to refuse her husband sexually, birth control, increased economic opportunities for women, and the right of women to serve on juries.

Quotes from Elizabeth Cady Stanton

The best protection any woman can have... is courage.

Self-development is a higher duty than self-sacrifice.

To throw obstacles in the way of a complete education is like putting out the eyes.

To make laws that man cannot, and will not obey, serves to bring all law into contempt.

---

[41] The temperance movement was a push to make the sale and consumption of alcohol illegal. The cause was especially appealing to women because alcohol was thought to be a major contributor to domestic violence.

Susan B. Anthony (1820-1906), Continuing the Revolution

(1) Susan B. Anthony was born in Massachusetts to a Quaker family. She attended Quaker boarding schools until the family experienced financial ruin during the Panic of 1837. At that time she began working as a teacher to help support the family.

(2) Susan B. Anthony was a supporter of the temperance movement throughout her career.

(3) After meeting Elizabeth Cady Stanton in 1851, Anthony began working for women's rights, especially the right to vote.

(4) From 1868 until 1870 Anthony and Stanton published a weekly magazine, *Revolution*, which discussed equal rights and social issues.

(5) In 1872 Anthony went to vote in her home town of Rochester, NY. Because she was famous and well respected, the poll workers allowed her to vote. Later she was arrested for voting illegally, tried, convicted, and fined. She refused to pay the fine and the government did not pursue the matter further.

(6) Anthony traveled extensively, making as many as 100 speeches a year.

(7) Susan B. Anthony remained single her entire life, saying that she would not be a slave to any man.

(8) Anthony celebrated her 80th birthday at the White House as a guest of President William McKinley.

(9) In 1979 the US mint began issuing the Susan B. Anthony dollar coin.

Quotes from Susan B. Anthony

Independence is happiness.

Men, their rights, and nothing more; women, their rights, and nothing less.

I distrust those people who know so well what God wants them to do, because I notice it always coincides with their own desires.

No man is good enough to govern any woman without her consent.

Elizabeth Blackwell (1821-1910) and the Dream of Medical School

(1)   Elizabeth Blackwell was born in 1821 into a large middle class merchant family in England. In 1832 the family immigrated to the United States.

(2)   Elizabeth's father supported the abolitionist movement in the US.

(3)   Elizabeth Blackwell's father died suddenly in 1838, leaving his large family in debt.

(4)   Elizabeth's sisters set-up a school for girls in Cincinnati shortly after their father died.

(5)   In 1844 Elizabeth Blackwell tried teaching in Kentucky, but she was unhappy in her rural setting and did not complete the school year.

(6)   In 1846 Blackwell tried teaching again, this time in South Carolina. She had now resolved that teaching was a temporary career while she saved money and prepared for medical school. She began reading and studying anatomy and medicine.

(7)   Elizabeth Blackwell had difficulty finding a medical school that would accept a female student. She was finally accepted at Geneva Medical College in New York in 1847. In 1849 Elizabeth Blackwell became the first woman to receive a medical degree in the United States.

(8)   After graduating medical school in the US, Elizabeth Blackwell went to Europe to continue her study of medicine in Paris and London. An eye infection caused by an accident while working in a hospital caused her to lose sight in one eye. This ended her hope of someday becoming a surgeon.

(9)   After Elizabeth Blackwell had opened the door for women in medicine, her sister, Emily, walked through it becoming the third woman doctor in the US. Together they opened The New York Infirmary for Indigent.[42]

(10)   Blackwell cofounded the London School of Medicine for Women in 1874.

(11)   Blackwell authored several books on topics close to her interests and work.

---

[42] Indigent: financially poor; empoverished.

Quotes from Elizabeth Blackwell

The idea of winning a doctor's degree gradually assumed the aspect of a great moral struggle, and the moral fight possessed immense attraction for me.

It is not easy to be a pioneer - but oh, it is fascinating!

If society will not admit of woman's free development, then society must be remodeled.

Our school education ignores, in a thousand ways, the rules of healthy development.

Margaret Sanger (1879-1966) and Birth Control

(1) Margaret Sanger was born Margaret Higgins in Corning, New York in 1879. Her mother gave birth to 11 children out of 18 pregnancies and died at age 49.

(2) Margaret began nurse's training in 1900 but quit before finishing when she married in 1902.

(3) In 1911 the Sanger family moved to New York City where Margaret worked as a visiting nurse in the slums of the East Side. Margaret became alarmed by the negative effects of frequent pregnancies on the lives and health of women with whom she worked.

(4) Margaret and her husband embraced socialist politics and activism. In 1911-1912 Margaret wrote a series of sex education articles, "What Every Mother Should Know," for the socialist magazine *New York Call,* then followed with another series in 1912-1913, "What Every Girl Should Know."

(5) Margaret Sanger continued to write about birth control in defiance of federal and state obscenity laws.

(6) In 1914, Sanger was convicted of sending birth control information through the mail, and she fled to England.

(7) In 1916 Sanger opened the first birth control clinic in United States in Brooklyn, New York. She was arrested for distributing

birth control devices and operating a public nuisance. She was convicted, lost her first appeal, but won a later appeal. During this time, the Sanger case did a great deal to move the birth control discussion forward.

(8) Sanger's birth control advocacy emphasized contraception as a much better alternative than the back street abortions which were common in the early 20th century. Her conflicts with the law were over "obscenity laws" which defined open discussion of birth control as obscene and illegal and prohibitions of the sale of contraceptive devices. She was not opposed to abortion in all cases, but she was not an advocate of abortion.

(9) Sanger remained an ardent advocate of free speech throughout her life.

Quotes from Margaret Sanger

Woman must have her freedom, the fundamental freedom of choosing whether or not she will be a mother and how many children she will have.

No woman can call herself free who does not own and control her body.

Diplomats make it their business to conceal the facts, and politicians violently denounce the politicians of other countries.

CHAPTER 11

POPULISM, PROGRESSIVISM, AND A PLACE ON THE WORLD STAGE

The Populists

Though the American economy was growing at a phenomenal rate in the late 19th century, many Americans were not sharing in the benefits. Henry Ford's "$5 per day" wage helped raise the general level of industrial wages in the early 20th century as other employers were forced to compete, but American farmers were being increasingly squeezed, and the majority of Americans still made their living by farming.

The main problem was that farmers felt compelled to invest in more heavy equipment to compete with each other. As a result of their use of technology, farms became more productive, but with more food being produced, the price of food continued to decrease. So, farmers had to invest more in equipment and produce more to earn the same amount they had earned before. Many farmers grew deeper and deeper in debt. Their plight was compounded by "price gouging" by the railroads.[43] Railroads could do this because most farms were served by only one rail line. Many farmers became very angry with the railroads.

To help relieve some of the pressure they were feeling, farmers began to advocate for government action to raise the general level of prices,

---

[43] Price gouging: charging a very high price for a good or service by someone who may be the only available supplier.

thereby allowing farm revenue to increase.[44] For prices to increase, the amount of money in circulation would have to increase. Nineteenth century law made this impossible because the government was prohibited from issuing any more money than could be backed up by the amount of gold in storage. The dollar was a "gold certificate", which meant that anyone could (at least in theory) exchange a dollar for a dollar's worth of gold. A political movement known as the "populist movement" grew in the late 19th century and the People's Party was formed around 1894. Most populists were farmers who wanted the government to abandon the "gold standard" and allow the dollar or be backed by gold or silver— "bimetallism." They also wanted regulation of the railroads. The party was absorbed into the Democratic Party in 1896 when the Democrats nominated Peoples' Party leader, William Jennings Bryan, for president.

William Jennings Bryan (1860-1925) and the Cross of Gold

(1)   The Nebraskan politician, William Jennings Bryan, became the universally accepted spokesman for the populist movement and the People's Party.

(2)   Bryan is most famous for his "Cross of Gold" speech to the Democratic National Convention in 1896. In this speech Bryan likened the "gold standard" to the cross on which Jesus is believed to have been crucified. The "gold standard" limited the amount of currency (money) in the US economy to the amount of gold held in the treasury at a time when farmers were producing more and incurring more debt. The general effect on farmers was that they had to produce more to compete, which meant going into debt to purchase more machinery, but as they produced more, prices farmer were receiving were decreasing.

---

[44] Revenue: the amount of money coming in as the result of sales.

When the general level of prices increase, that is called "inflation." Inflation is usually considered a bad thing, but many economists argue that a small, managed amount of inflation can be helpful at least at times.

(3)   Bryan and the Populist proposed that the government accept both gold and silver as payment for dollars (bimetallism) to allow the currency to grow with the increased productivity in the economy.

(4)   In 1896 Bryan was nominated for president by three political parties—the Democrats, the Populists (People's Party), and the Silver Republicans.

(5)   Bryan's nomination for president by the Democratic Party in 1896, made him the youngest person ever nominated for president by a major political Party. He was 36 years old.

(6)   William Jennings Bryan was the Democratic nominee for president three times— in 1896, 1900, and 1908. He was never elected President.

(7)   Bryan volunteered for service during the Spanish-American War (1898). He was commissioned a colonel in the Nebraska militia, but did not see combat.

(8)   As a politician, Bryan opposed the concentration of wealth and power by the banks, insurance companies, and railroads. He was also generally anti-war, and a promoter of the prohibition of alcohol.[45]

(9)   William Jennings Bryan served as Secretary of State under President Woodrow Wilson from 1913 until 1915. He resigned in a dispute with Wilson over an appropriate US response to the 1915 sinking of the Lusitania by a German U boat (submarine).

(10)   The Cowardly Lion in the Wizard of Oz is thought to have been modeled on Bryan. America did enter World War I, but not until April 1917. So, the US was actively engaged in the war for about one year at a cost of about 100,000 American lives. The other major combatants—England, France, Germany, Austria-Hungary, and Russia—all had much larger losses. The war dragged on for over four years.

---

[45] Prohibition (from the root word prohibit): The prohibition movement sought to prohibit the sale and consumption of alcohol in the United States. Prohibitionists, like Bryan, succeeded in passing the 18th Amendment to the Constitution. The experiment failed though and the Prohibition Amendment became the only Constitutional Amendment ever repealed.

(11) Bryan was deeply religious. Because of his religious convictions, he became involved in the famous "Scopes Monkey Trial" of 1925.[46] Bryan took the witness stand as an expert witness. The defense attorney, Clarence Darrow, was able to embarrass Bryan by proving that Bryan had little grasp of history from Biblical times. Bryan died five days after the verdict was announced.

Quotes from William Jennings Bryan

Destiny is no matter of chance. It is a matter of choice. It is not a thing to be waited for, it is a thing to be achieved.

The way to develop self-confidence is to do the thing you fear and get a record of successful experiences behind you.

Eloquent speech is not from lip to ear, but rather from heart to heart.

The Progressives

The Progressive movement in the United States began near the end of the 19th century. Many progressive leaders, such as Jane Addams, John Dewey, Theodore Roosevelt, and Woodrow Wilson, were urban and well educated.[47] Progressives wanted (1) more professionalism in government and (2) more democracy. Many progressives were also concerned about improving the lives of the urban poor and breaking the power of large monopoly corporations to set artificially high prices.

Most of the best known progressive reforms were at the state level. Wisconsin Governor (later Senator) Robert La Follette was at the forefront of early progressive programs. Progressive practices which have become part of government and politics in many states today include the following.

Initiative—By the initiative process, the people can propose and pass a law. The process begins with a petition. If the petition receives the

---

[46] Scopes Monkey Trial: This trial came about because a high school biology teacher was dismissed (fired) for teaching the theory of evolution which state law had prohibited. The Supreme Court ruled that teaching the theory of evolution cannot be prohibited.

[47] Urban: belong to a city, usually a larger city.

required number of valid signatures of registered voters, the provision is placed on the ballot for a direct vote of the people.

Referendum—By the referendum process the legislature can propose to have the people vote directly on a law.

Recall—If the state has a recall mechanism, citizens can call for a special election if they are unhappy with an official and wish to remove him/her from office before the official end of his/her term.

Direct Primary Elections—These are very common today in most states. This process takes the nominating procedure away from the political parties. Voters decide who the party nominees will be.

City (or County) Manager Government—Many big cities have embraced this idea. The manager is not elected, but rather he/she is a hired professional with specific managerial skills.

Most of the progressive reforms mentioned above have a negative side. For example, recall elections have proven to be unnecessarily costly. The question then becomes, do the positive effects outweigh the negatives?

Four important Constitutional Amendments also came out of the Progressive movement. These are:

The 16th Amendment (1913)—established a national income tax.

The 17th Amendment (1913)—provided for the direct election of US Senators. Prior to this Senators were selected by state legislatures. The system of selection could be easily corrupted because rich candidates would only have to buy a limited number of votes to be elected. Prior to the 17th Amendment the Senate was sometimes jokingly referred to as "the millionaires' club."

The 18th Amendment (1913)—prohibited the sale and consumption of alcohol. This was a failed experiment. Many Americans resented and flaunted this law.[48] The greatest long-term (and unexpected) result was that organized crime evolved to serve the market for illegal booze. This **18th Amendment** was repealed by the **20th Amendment (1933)**. This was the only amendment ever repealed.

The 19th Amendment (1920)—Guaranteed women the right to vote. Prior to this amendment the states decided this, and women were not allowed to vote in most states.

---

[48] Flaunt: to openly exaggerate an action. To "flaunt a law" is to openly disobey it. During "Prohibition" many people took pleasure in drinking alcohol at "Speak Easies", semi-secret alcohol bars.

Robert "Fighting Bob" La Follette, Sr. (1855-1925) and the Wisconsin Idea

(1) Wisconsin Governor Robert La Follette, Sr. established what became known as "the Wisconsin Idea" by working closely with the University of Wisconsin to develop progressive reforms. La Follette became the unofficial early leader of the progressive movement and an influential member of the Progressive Party formed by Theodore Roosevelt in 1912.

(2) Robert La Follette's father died in 1856. His mother remarried, and he had a difficult relationship with his step-father.

(3) Robert La Follette began his political career by serving three terms in the US House of Representatives, but he was defeated for reelection in 1890.

(4) La Follette served as governor of Wisconsin from 1901 to 1906.

(5) La Follette ran for president in the Republican Primary Elections of 1912 and won two states—his home state of Wisconsin and North Dakota.

(6) La Follette ran again for president in 1924 as the Progressive Party candidate. The Party had been formed in 1912 by the charismatic Theodore Roosevelt. By 1924 it no longer had much popular support. "Fighting Bob" La Follette won only his home state of Wisconsin.

(7) Robert La Follette, Sr. served in the US Senate from 1907 until his death in 1925.

(8) La Follette is considered by historians and politicians to have been one of America's greatest Senators.

(9) Robert La Follette, Sr. is one of only six Senators whose portraits hang in the reception room of the US Senate.

(10) Robert La Follette, Sr. was popularly known as "Fighting Bob" for opposing the control of the Wisconsin Republican Party by wealthy donors.

(11) La Follette championed the cause of indigenous-Americans and African-Americans.

(12) La Follette unsuccessfully opposed US entry into World War I, but he successfully opposed US membership in the League of Nations. He was very anti-war.

(13) A statue of Robert La Follette, Sr. is one of the two statues representing Wisconsin in the National Statuary Hall in Washington, DC.

(14) The University of Wisconsin's School of Public Affairs is the Robert La Follette School.

Quotes from Robert La Follette, Sr.

Every nation has its war party... It is commercial, imperialistic, ruthless. It tolerates no opposition.

In times of peace, the war party insists on making preparation for war. As soon as prepared for, it insists on making war.

Jane Addams (1860-1935) and Hull House

(1) Jane Addams is one of the greatest social reformers of the twentieth century.

(2) Jane Addams is most famous for establishing Hull House, a complex which helped the poor, especially newly arrived immigrants, in Chicago. Hull House was a resource for aid, education, and culture.

(3) Jane was the youngest of eight children. Jane's mother died when Jane was two years old. Three siblings died in infancy, and one sibling died at age 16.

(4) Jane contracted tuberculosis at age four. Other health complications left her with a permanently curved spine. She also walked with a slight limp. Growing up she felt ugly and somewhat embarrassed by her physical problems.

(5) Addams studied medicine for one year, but was forced to leave school because of health problems and a nervous breakdown.

(6) Jane Addams wrote several books of social commentary about her time. Her most famous book is the autobiography, *Twenty Years at Hull House*.

(7) Jane Addams directed Hull House based on her own "three ethical principles": **One,** teach by example; **two,** practice cooperation; and **three,** practice egalitarian democracy.[49]

(8) Jane Addams turned down offers of appointments to university faculty positions in order to remain independent.

(9) Jane Addams refused to align herself with any ideological movement (like the feminist movement of her time), preferring pragmatism.[50]

(10) Addams was a charter member of both the American Sociological Society and the NAACP.

(11) Jane Addams was selected to officially nominate Theodore Roosevelt for president during the Progressive Party Convention of 1912.

(12) Addams opposed American entry into World War I, but supported proposed American membership in the League of Nations.

(13) From the beginning of World War I until the end of her life, Jane Addams concentrated her efforts on opposing war. She was awarded the Nobel Peace Prize in 1931. She is the only American woman to have been so honored.

(14) Jane Addams was an associate of the great American philosopher and educator, John Dewey. She consulted with him in developing her philosophy of social ethics. Both Addams and Dewey taught that democracy is as much about duty as it is about individualism.

Quotes from Jane Addams

Civilization is a method of living, an attitude of equal respect for all men.

The essence of immorality is the tendency to make an exception of myself.

Action indeed is the sole medium of expression for ethics.

---

[49] Egalitarian: emphasis on total equality and rejection of class differences among people.

[50] Pragmatism: a philosophy which emphasizes seeking desired ends by the most efficient methods.

Theodore Roosevelt (1859-1919), a Progressive with a Big Stick, US President 1901-1909

(1) Theodore Roosevelt is one of the four US presidents immortalized with his image on the famous Mount Rushmore sculpture. The four images on Mount Rushmore are George Washington, Thomas Jefferson, Abraham Lincoln, and Theodore Roosevelt. Theodore is still considered to have been one of America's greatest presidents. His activist approach changed the nature of the presidency. His progressivism led eventually to a progressive trend in American presidential politics. And his conservationism, years ahead of his time, made him revered as America's only great conservationist president.

(2) As a young boy, Theodore was weak and sickly. He had severe bouts of asthma and was physically frail. His asthma was so severe that he sometimes felt that he might die from inability to breathe. But he refused to accept this condition, and set about developing his body through increasingly strenuous physical training.

(3) Theodore Roosevelt was already an expert ornithologist (person who studies birds) by the time he began his studies at Harvard. Theodore had been home schooled, and he read a great deal on a variety of subjects of particular interest to him. By the time he began his university studies, he was seriously considering a career as an ornithologist. Because he had put a great deal of energy into his studies, Roosevelt was already knowledgeable in several fields when entering Harvard. He also had a passion for history.

(4) Roosevelt finished as the runner-up (second place) in the Harvard student boxing tournament one year. The sickly, asthmatic boy had transformed himself into a vigorous, physically fit young man. He remained thus for the rest of his life and is often thought to have been the most physically fit of all American presidents.

(5) Theodore's wife and mother both died in the same house, on the same day, Valentine's Day, 1884.

Roosevelt's young wife had just given birth to a daughter on February 12. She had had a difficult pregnancy. The doctors had failed to detect a life threatening illness. Immediately after giving birth Alice Roosevelt became seriously ill. Theodore, who was away serving in the New York state legislature, rushed home to find both his wife and his mother dying. He spent what must have been an agonizing night trying to help and comfort both women. The next day he wrote in his diary, "The light has gone out of my life." One friend noted that Theodore was close to a breakdown.

Roosevelt went back to Albany to finish off the current legislative term. Then he went to Dakota Territory where he had purchased a ranch. There he remade himself and, through the toughness and determination he exhibited, won the respect of the cowboys with whom he associated. He also learned to respect and understand them. Years later he famously said that if he had not gone to Dakota then he would never have become president. The daughter, whom Theodore named Alice after her mother, had been left with Theodore's sister to raise for the time being.

(6)   Roosevelt failed as a rancher then returned to New York City to run for mayor and came in third.

Roosevelt's failure in Dakota Territory was due to no fault of his own. He and many other ranchers in the region were wiped out when most of their cattle froze to death in the coldest winter ever known in the territory.

Despite his misfortune, Roosevelt came out of this experience with renewed confidence in his own abilities to adapt, hold his own among the rugged men of the west, and thrive. He also wrote three popular books about his experiences as a rancher.

(7)   Theodore Roosevelt first gained fame as a writer. TR wrote many books and hundreds of articles. His most famous works include his two volume *History of the Naval War of 1812*, which was critically acclaimed in both the US and Britain, and a four volume frontier history, *The Winning of the West*, which was very popular in its time.

(8) Theodore hated to be called "Teddy." Although "Teddy" or "Ted" are the commonly acceptable shortened forms of "Theodore" in American English, Roosevelt always insisted that he was "Theodore" or simply "TR." TR defined himself; he refused to be defined by others.

(9) Theodore Roosevelt's "Rough Rider" regiment is the most famous single regiment in US military history. While serving as Assistant Secretary of the Navy in 1898, Roosevelt was pushing for war with Spain in support of a revolution in Cuba (and as a way of acquiring an American empire). War was declared when the *USS Maine* blew up in Havana Harbor, killing more than 200 crewmen. We know now that an internal explosion in the boiler room of the ship caused the accident, but Roosevelt and others blamed Spain and demanded war. To his credit, when war was declared, Roosevelt insisted that he must go and fight, himself, in this war which he had promoted.

Believing that western cowboys would be naturally suited to serve as cavalry troops in Cuba, he proposed a regiment be recruited from the territories of the southwest—Arizona, New Mexico, Oklahoma, and the Indian Territory. But Roosevelt had many connections in New York City and through Harvard. A number of "Eastern dudes" were also accepted into this "cowboy" regiment. Roosevelt's men were officially designated as the "First United States Volunteer Cavalry," but the press invented the now famous name "Roosevelt's Rough Riders."

(10) The war was short and the Rough Riders were actually involved in only two battles. But because Roosevelt was famous and would generate interesting stories, much of the press followed and reported on the Rough Riders. Roosevelt returned to the US as the hero of the Spanish-American War.

(11) Roosevelt was actually second in command of the Rough Riders until the day they made their famous charge up San Juan Hill. Roosevelt's close friend, Colonel Leonard Wood, a professional soldier, actually commanded the Rough Riders. Roosevelt was

second in command as a Lieutenant Colonel. In Cuba, tropical diseases soon caused restructuring of command. On the eve of the assault on San Juan Heights, Wood was promoted to command all cavalry troops. At that time, Roosevelt was promoted to full command of the Rough Riders.

(12) Colonel Roosevelt was the only "Rough Rider" to ride a horse in Cuba. Troop transport to Cuba was very limited and disorganized. The Rough Riders were not even able to secure transport for all of the men. (About 1/3 of the Rough Riders were left behind in Florida when the boat sailed.) Only two horses were taken along—both were Roosevelt's. "Roosevelt's Rough Riders" joked among themselves that they had been demoted from "Roosevelt's Rough Riders" to "Wood's Weary Walkers."

(13) Roosevelt was recommended for the Congressional Medal of Honor for his actions in the Battle of San Juan Hill in 1898.

The famous "Battle of San Juan Hill" was actually a full assault by the entire American army in Cuba on the long ridge of San Juan Heights overlooking Santiago harbor. The Rough Riders were only part of the assault, but many of the war correspondents attached themselves to Roosevelt's regiment.

In the battle, the Rough Riders had to first gain control of the lower part of the ridge, a place called Kettle Hill. Roosevelt led the assault on Kettle Hill conspicuously as the only man on horseback, making himself an easy and prominent target for Spanish fire. This is the part of the assault for which Roosevelt gained the recommendation for the Medal in recognition of his conspicuous bravery.

But Roosevelt's superiors decided to deny him the Medal alleging that TR's bravery was in the line of duty and not a great deal more than that of others involved in the battle.

About the time of the centennial (100 year) anniversary of the battle, a campaign was begun to have the Medal awarded posthumously. And so the Congressional Medal of Honor was added to the accolades of Theodore Roosevelt in 2001.

(14) TR was America's youngest president. Vice-president Theodore Roosevelt came to the presidency at the age of 42 upon the death of President William McKinley. John F. Kennedy was 43 when he became president. Kennedy was the youngest man elected president.

Roosevelt had ascended quickly through the political ranks after the Spanish-American War as the result of his new status as a war hero. He returned to New York in August and was elected governor in November. By 1900 the New York Republican Party had become unhappy with Roosevelt because they could not control him. They wanted to move him into a position where he would never be heard from again. Their solution was to manipulate Roosevelt into the vice-presidency. When he was elected, one of the New York bosses is known to have said, "Doesn't anyone know that there's only one life between that madman and the White House." A few months later, President McKinley was assassinated and the same New York party boss lamented, "Now that damn cowboy is president."

(15) Theodore Roosevelt named his presidency the "Square Deal." By this he meant that all people would be considered equal. The time of special privilege for big business would end. Early in Roosevelt's administration a coal strike threatened to turn into a national disaster. Previous presidents had tended to intervene in strikes in favor of the big companies. Roosevelt refused to do this and pressured the mining company to settle when he saw that it was refusing to deal fairly with the union.

Later he began the practice of enforcing the Sherman Anti-trust Act against monopolies as had been intended, and he became known as the "Trust Buster."

Though TR was a Republican, the tradition of naming the presidential administration caught on among Democratic presidents. Theodore's cousin Franklin Roosevelt called his administration the "New Deal." Harry Truman had the "Fair Deal." John F. Kennedy dubbed his time the "New Frontier." And Lyndon Johnson strove for the "Great Society."

(16) Theodore Roosevelt coined the term "Bully Pulpit" for the office of the presidency, referring to what he saw as his responsibilities to speak-up for justice and, thereby, use the power of the presidency to apply pressure in favor of causes he valued.

(17) TR was the first president to host a black man at dinner in the White House. Roosevelt did share the erroneous racial beliefs of his time, but his mind was open enough to appreciate and accept any individual who had proven himself to be a person of value. Booker T. Washington, the first black person to dine at the White House, was a person of value.

(18) TR was the first US president to ride in an airplane. He was also the first US president to ride in a submarine. However, TR was not the first US president to ride in an automobile. That was his predecessor, William McKinley. McKinley was taken by auto/ ambulance to a hospital where he died from an assassin's bullet.

(19) TR gave away the bride in the wedding of Franklin and Eleanor Roosevelt. Eleanor Roosevelt was the daughter of TR's only brother. That brother, Eliot Roosevelt, had died years earlier. Franklin was a distant cousin. A humorous story is told of when the newlywed couple first visited TR in the White House. TR is purported to have asked young Franklin what he thought of the place. To which Franklin replied that he liked it very much and he should like to live there some day.

(20) The Teddy Bear is named for Theodore Roosevelt. Roosevelt had been bear hunting one day with no luck at all. His party had seen no trace of a bear until one man stumbled onto a cub (baby bear), threw a rope around its neck, and dragged it over to the President so that he could shoot it. Roosevelt of course refused and told the man to let it go. The news of the event made the

papers and someone saw the opportunity to profit from the story by inventing the Teddy Bear.

(21) President Roosevelt knowingly appointed an ex-convict as US Marshal for Arizona Territory.

Roosevelt was constantly deluged by former Rough Riders with request for jobs. One such request came from Benjamin Daniels in Arizona. Daniels had impressed Roosevelt as a soldier enough to be praised specifically by Colonel Roosevelt in his book, *Rough Riders*. Daniels also had an impressive resume as a lawman. This included several years as Assistant City Marshal of Dodge City, Kansas during the 1880s when the town was famous as a "wild west" town.

During Daniels' confirmation hearing in Washington a slew of accusations from burglary and armed robbery to murder were brought before the Senate. But when the former mayor of Dodge City was contacted by the Senate, he provided a glowing account of Daniels' performance as an officer.

When the worst of the charges had been answered Roosevelt asked Daniels if there was anything else. Daniels replied that there was nothing else, whereupon, the President issued another hearty endorsement of his friend. Then the bomb dropped. The Senate was informed that Ben Daniels had spent three years in a federal prison for the theft of government mules. Roosevelt confronted Daniels about this and Daniels made the very weak excuse that he had forgotten about those three years. An embarrassed Roosevelt withdrew the nomination.

But the story did not end there; it just began to become interesting. Roosevelt wrote a long letter to Daniels encouraging him to take his disappointment like a man and act with integrity from that time forward, hinting that his friends might still be able to help him if he stayed straight.

About a year later Roosevelt helped arrange a position for Daniels. Daniels became the Superintendent of the Arizona Territorial

Prison at Yuma. (Daniels did have prison experience after all.) After Daniels had proven himself by exemplary work as a prison superintendent, Roosevelt again quietly submitted Daniels' name for the marshal position in Arizona and Daniels was quickly confirmed. Roosevelt had gambled his own reputation on the Daniels he had known in Cuba. Was Daniels really worthy of the risk Roosevelt took for him?

Daniels proved himself to be fiercely loyal to Roosevelt and took care to act in a way to bring honor to himself and the President. By the time the marshal had completed his term, Roosevelt was extolling the fine record of Marshal Daniels as among the best in the nation.

Daniels had been redeemed through the faith Roosevelt had placed in him. Such is the redemptive power of the faith of one human being in another. But Roosevelt could only provide the opportunity, Daniels had to make good himself after that.

(22) TR lost the site in one eye while boxing in the White House. This fact was concealed from the general public.

(23) President Theodore Roosevelt read Upton Sinclair's book, *The Jungle*, and reported that it almost made him sick. He then directed Congress to make needed reforms. The results were the *Pure Food and Drug Act*, which established the Food and Drug Administration, and the *Meat Inspection Act*.

(24) Theodore Roosevelt was the first American president to receive the Nobel Peace Prize. Roosevelt acted as a mediator to end a war between Russia and Japan in 1905. For this he was given the Nobel Peace Prize. This is ironic because Roosevelt's critics often accused him of war mongering.

(25) TR made the expression "speak softly and carry a big stick" famous. This was actually an African expression, but Roosevelt liked it and made it something of the theme of his foreign policy. He famously exerted American power in support of the independence of Panama from Columbia when negotiations with

Columbia to build the Panama Canal broke down. This and other Roosevelt "big stick" policies remain somewhat controversial.

(26) When Venezuela and the Dominican Republic became heavily indebted to European countries and were unable to pay, those countries were threatened with European invasion. In response to this threat, President Roosevelt issued the "Roosevelt Corollary" to the "Monroe Doctrine."[51] By this new interpretation of Monroe, America would take it upon itself to intervene when necessary in the Americas to keep order and thereby eliminate any temptation for any other foreign power to intervene.

(27) After leaving office in 1909, former President Roosevelt went on a killing spree in Africa in the guise of a safari to obtain specimens for the Museum of Natural History in New York City. Theodore Roosevelt and his son Kermit killed a total of more than 500 animals on this trip: 17 lions, 11 elephants, 20 rhinoceroses, 9 giraffes, 47 gazelles, 8 hippopotamuses, 29 zebras, 9 hyenas, and a wide variety of other animals. The number of animals killed is shocking. The excuse was that these animals would all be donated to the New York Museum of Natural History for display.

(28) After being out of office for four years, TR attempted to win back the White House in 1912. In announcing his candidacy for the Republican nomination, Roosevelt coined a phrase by saying, "I'm throwing my hat into the ring." He won nine of the thirteen Republican primary elections held that year. President Taft won two and Robert La Follette won two. Roosevelt was angry when he was denied the nomination at the party convention. He then formed his own third party.

Progressivism was a reform political movement in the early twentieth century which found many adherents in both major political parties. Roosevelt attempted to rally progressives from both parties into his Progressive Party. But the Democratic Party countered the movement by nominating the very progressive

---

[51] Corollary: a proposition which flows from one already established.

Woodrow Wilson for president.[52] The result was that Roosevelt split the Republican Party vote without gaining any significant support from Democrats. With the Republican vote split, Wilson was elected. He was only the second Democrat to be elected president since the Civil War. Roosevelt finished second. Poor President Taft finished a distant (and humiliating) third.

(29) When asked in 1912 if he felt strong enough for another run for the Presidency, Roosevelt responded that he was as strong as a Bull Moose. As a result, the Progressive Party of 1912 also became known as the Bull Moose Party.

(30) Theodore Roosevelt once gave an hour long speech between being shot in an assassination attempt and going to the hospital. During the Presidential campaign of 1912 in Milwaukee as Roosevelt was preparing to give a speech there, he was shot in the chest. Then he insisted on giving his full speech before going to the hospital.

(31) A long, mysterious river in Brazil is named for Theodore Roosevelt. After losing the presidential election of 1912, Roosevelt set out for adventure. He headed an expedition to explore a portion of the Amazon River known as the River of Doubt. After that expedition, the River of Doubt was renamed "Rio Roosevelt." The expedition was quite perilous. Roosevelt became injured and ill and almost died. This probably shortened Roosevelt's life. He never fully recovered all the vigor he had before the expedition. He died in January 1919 at the age of only 60.

Quotes from Theodore Roosevelt

Keep your eyes on the stars, and your feet on the ground.

Believe you can and you're halfway there.

In any moment of decision, the best thing you can do is the right thing, the next best thing is the wrong thing, and the worst thing you can do is nothing.

---

[52] Woodrow Wilson was progressive on every issue except for race. Born and raised in Virginia, he could not transcend his background.

If you could kick the person in the pants responsible for most of your trouble, you wouldn't sit for a month.

Far better is it to dare mighty things, to win glorious triumphs, even though checkered by failure... than to rank with those poor spirits who neither enjoy nor suffer much, because they live in a gray twilight that knows not victory nor defeat.

With self-discipline most anything is possible.

Great thoughts speak only to the thoughtful mind, but great actions speak to all mankind.

The most important single ingredient in the formula of success is knowing how to get along with people.

Far and away the best prize that life has to offer is the chance to work hard at work worth doing.

Nobody cares how much you know, until they know how much you care.

Do what you can, with what you have, where you are.

Big jobs usually go to the men who prove their ability to outgrow small ones.

The only man who never makes a mistake is the man who never does anything.

To educate a man in mind and not in morals is to educate a menace to society.

Character, in the long run, is the decisive factor in the life of an individual and of nations alike.

I think there is only one quality worse than hardness of heart and that is softness of head.

(Thomas) Woodrow Wilson (1856-1924), Progressive Idealist, US President 1912-1920

(1) Thomas Woodrow Wilson was known to the public simply as Woodrow Wilson. He was elected President in 1912 and promoted progressive reforms throughout his first term.

(2) Woodrow Wilson was affected by dyslexia and had trouble learning to read as a result.[53]

(3) Wilson was born and raised in the south. In 1912 he became the first man with a southern background to be elected President since before the Civil War. Though he is considered to be a "progressive", his ideas about race were not enlightened.

(4) Woodrow Wilson was primarily an academic.[54] His career was as a university professor and the President of Princeton University.

(5) In 1912 Wilson's only prior active governmental position was one two year term as governor of New Jersey.

(6) Wilson won the 1912 Presidential election with only about 40% of the popular vote because the Republican vote was split between Incumbent President William Howard Taft and the Progressive Party candidate, former President Theodore Roosevelt. (The last President elected with only 40% before this was Abraham Lincoln in 1860.)

(7) President Wilson was the first US President since Thomas Jefferson to deliver a live State of the Union Speech to Congress.

(8) President Wilson's first wife died during his first term, and he remarried about a year later.

(9) President Wilson was a progressive Democrat. Many progressive laws were enacted during his first term. The best known of these include: The Federal Reserve Act, The Federal Trade Commission Act, The Clayton Anti-trust Act, and the Federal Farm Act.

(10) Under President Wilson, the US Navy occupied the Mexican port of Vera Cruz for seven month beginning in April 1914. This action was taken to enforce an embargo of weapons from the

[53] Dyslexia: the tendency to see things backward out of the given order in one's mind.
[54] Academic: professional scholar.

US at this point in the Mexican Revolution, as President Wilson was opposed to the regime of Victoriano Huerta, who had seized power.

(11) After Mexican revolutionary Francisco "Pancho" Villa raided Columbus, New Mexico, killing 17 Americans, President Wilson sent General John J. "Black Jack" Pershing into northern Mexico to capture or kill Villa. Pershing's men chased Villa for 11 month and killed many of Villa's men in skirmishes, but Villa alluded capture.

(12) World War I began in 1914. To President Wilson's credit, he kept the US out of the war for three full years. The war was a disastrous blood bath. Germany lost 2 million combatants killed; France had losses of 1.4 million; Austria-Hungary lost 1.4 million soldiers; the UK wasted 900,000 young men; the Ottoman Empire lost a half million; and Russia suffered 2 million killed, even though it pulled out of the war in 1917. Some of the minor combatants also suffered staggering losses: Italy lost a half a million; Romania sacrificed 300,000; and Serbia, where the war started, lost 400,000 of its soldiers. US losses of more than 100,000 are tragic, but could have been much worse.

Woodrow Wilson won a second term as President with the slogan "he kept us out of war," but shortly after Wilson's second inauguration he asked Congress for a declaration of war on Germany. Unrestricted submarine warfare by Germany and a provocative telegram sent by Germany and intended for Mexico were the stated causes of the request. British intelligence had intercepted the telegram in which the German government encouraged Mexico to declare war on the United States.

(13) President Wilson had highly idealistic war aims. He said that we were going to war to "make the world safe for democracy" and that this would be the "war to end all wars."

(14) President Wilson was intolerant of dissension during the war. He had Congress enact laws making criticism of the war effort a crime.

(15) A deadly pandemic of influenza began in 1918.[55] It would sweep across the earth and kill an estimated 20 million worldwide. The majority of the Americans who died during World War I did not die from combat but rather from influenza.

(16) President Wilson proposed "14 points" as the basis for a permanent peace agreement. Germany capitulated with the expectation that the peace would be based on the 14 points.[56] But the victorious allies—the UK, France, and Italy—refused the stipulations.

(17) The core of Wilson's plan for permanent world peace was an international organization. This was the only provision of the 14 points enacted. The League of Nations was created.

(18) Congress rejected US membership in the League of Nations fearing that such membership would commit the US to intervene in future European conflicts. The US never joined the League of Nations.

(19) With Congress opposed to the US membership in the League of Nations, President Wilson toured the country by train to try to promote support for the League. While on this tour, he suffered a stroke and was mostly incapacitated and sequestered[57] for the remaining year of his presidency. There is speculation that the President's wife was running the country during much of this time.

(20) Wilson's own stubbornness contributed to his failure to achieve his goals. He had refused to include leading Republicans in the Versailles negotiations.

Quotes from Thomas Woodrow Wilson

You are not here merely to make a living. You are here in order to enable the world to live more amply, with greater vision, with a finer spirit of hope and achievement. You are here to enrich the world, and you impoverish yourself if you forget the errand.

---

[55] Pandemic: a large scale outbreak of disease worldwide.
[56] Capitulate: agree to stop fighting, essentially to surrender.
[57] Sequestered: isolated

The thing to do is to supply light and not heat.

There is no higher religion than human service. To work for the common good is the greatest creed.

I would rather lose in a cause that will someday win, than win in a cause that will someday lose.

PART 3

1920 THROUGH 1945, A NEW SUPERPOWER IN A CHANGED WORLD

The "war to end all wars" of course did nothing of the sort, but really only disillusioned people in America and Europe. The 1920s became the era of the "lost generation."[58] The immense sacrifices of the "Great War" now seemed meaningless.[59] Republican Warren Gamliel Harding won the US Presidency in 1920 with his proposal to "return to normalcy", and both Americans and Europeans seemed to just want to live for the moment and enjoy life. The meaninglessness of life was a common literary theme in popular novels such as *The Great Gatsby* by F. Scott Fitzgerald and Ernest Hemingway's premier novel, *The Sun Also Rises*.

The social phenomenon known as the Harlem Renaissance is identified with the 1920s, but a more accurate time frame for this would extend into the 1930s. This is also true to some extent of the term the "Jazz Age."

A crisis of faith began in the 1920s and peaked in the 1930s with the Great Depression. The Depression lasted a decade, and 25% of the US labor force was unemployed at its height. The Depression really only ended

---

[58] "The Lost Generation": the generation of young men who served in the Great War and returned disillusioned and jaded. The term was popularized by Ernest Hemingway in his novel, *The Sun Also Rises*. Hemingway credited Gertrude Stein with teaching him the term.

[59] The Great War: this was what the European war of 1914 to 1918 was called until we had World War II.

when governments were forced to engage in massive deficit spending in order to fund combat efforts in World War II.[60]

If there was ever a just war, World War II was that; a war to defeat evil, the evils of Nazism, Fascism, and military expansionism. 1945 was America's shining time. The US emerged from the war as the moral leader of the world, but it was not the only superpower.

---

[60] Deficit spending: spending whereby expenditures (money spent) exceeds revenues (money coming in).

CHAPTER 12

THE ROARING 20S AKA THE JAZZ AGE, THE HARLEM RENAISSANCE, AND THE CRASH, 1920-1930[61]

F. Scott Fitzgerald (1896-1940), Explaining a Generation

(1) F. Scott Fitzgerald's greatest novel, *The Great Gatsby*, defined the confused, restless, unfocused generation of the Jazz Age, but this novel was not popular until after Fitzgerald's death.

(2) F. Scott Fitzgerald was born in Minnesota and raised in New York State. He wanted to be a writer from an early age. His first published story was in his school newspaper when he was 13 years old.

(3) F. Scott Fitzgerald attended Princeton University.

(4) Fitzgerald served in the US army in the Great War and was commissioned as a lieutenant, but the war ended before he could be sent to serve in combat.

(5) Though Fitzgerald preferred to write novels, he could not support his wife and child on his earnings from novels. He often borrowed money from friends. His greatest commercial success during his lifetime came from writing magazine articles.

---

[61] Aka: also known as.

(6)   Fitzgerald lived in Paris in the 1920s and was part of the literary group which gathered regularly in the home of Gertrude Stein and included Ernest Hemingway.

(7)   F. Scott Fitzgerald and his wife, Zelda, did not have a happy life despite his fame. He battled his own alcoholism, and she battled mental illness. Zelda was institutionalized for much of her later short life, and Scott's alcoholism contributed to his early death.

(8)   F. Scott Fitzgerald moved to Hollywood in the late 1930s where he attempted screenwriting with limited success, but was able to continued publishing short stories.

Quotes from F. Scott Fitzgerald

Vitality shows in not only the ability to persist but the ability to start over.

Genius is the ability to put into effect what is on your mind.

First you take a drink, then the drink takes a drink, then the drink takes you.

Ernest Hemingway (1899-1961) and the Lost Generation

(1)   Ernest Hemingway lived in Paris for a time in the 1920s and was part of the group of literary figures who met regularly at the home of Gertrude Stein and included F. Scott Fitzgerald. They define and explain the Jazz Age.

(2)   Ernest Hemingway became interested in newspaper writing while in high school in Illinois.

(3)   Hemingway graduated from high school in 1917 and worked briefly as a newspaper reporter before enlisting to serve as an ambulance driver in Italy during the Great War.

(4)   Ernest Hemingway was seriously wounded and fell in love with a nurse while recovering in the hospital and probably used the experience as the basis for his later novel, *A Farewell to Arms*.

(5)   Hemingway's first novel, *The Sun Also Rises*, made the term "the lost generation" common, as descriptive of the young men

who had returned from the Great War with feelings of vague emptiness.

(6) Hemingway wrote short, clear, action sentences. His style of writing was revolutionary and had an immediate effect on how other writers would write.

(7) In 1937 Hemingway went to Spain to report on the Spanish Civil War. This experience was the source of his novel, *For Whom the Bell Tolls.*

(8) Hemingway was an adventurer who hunted in Africa and fished in the Florida Keys.

(9) Hemingway's story, *The Old Man and the Sea*, won the Nobel Prize for literature.

(10) Hemingway's life was not always happy. He was divorced three time (and married four times), and his death was by suicide.

Quotes from Ernest Hemingway

The best way to find out if you can trust somebody is to trust them.

There is nothing noble in being superior to your fellow men. True nobility lies in being superior to your former self.

Courage is grace under pressure.

The world breaks everyone, and afterward, some are strong at the broken places.

I like to listen. I have learned a great deal from listening carefully. Most people never listen.

Never mistake motion for action.

As you get older it is harder to have heroes, but it is sort of necessary.

(Edward K) "Duke" Ellington (1899-1974) and Jazz

(1)   Duke Ellington was born in Washington, DC in 1899. Both of his parents were pianists. He began piano lessons at age 7.

(2)   The Duke Ellington Orchestra was formed in 1923. The orchestra continued and performed regularly for over 50 years until Ellington's death in 1974.

(3)   The Duke Ellington Orchestra performed at the famous Cotton Club in Harlem, NY during the 1920s which made Ellington a leader of the Jazz Age and the Harlem Renaissance.

(4)   Jazz is a uniquely American art form which evolved from African-American roots to become popular throughout the world. Ellington preferred the term "American Music" to the term "jazz" for his work.

(5)   During his long career Ellington wrote more than 1,000 compositions.

(6)   The Duke Ellington Orchestra toured Europe during the 1930s and made a world tour in 1956.

Quotes from "Duke" Ellington

A problem is a chance for you to do your best.

I merely took the energy it takes to pout and wrote some blues.

(James M.) Langston Hughes (1902-1967), Renaissance Voice

(1)   (James M.) Langston Hughes is considered to have been among the most important writers of the Harlem Renaissance.

(2)   Langston Hughes was born in Joplin, Missouri in 1902. His parents divorced when he was young. His mother was a teacher who could not support the family on her own, so Langston went to live with his grandmother. In his adolescence and young

adulthood he bounce around between his father, his mother, and family friends.

(3)   Langston began writing poetry in grammar school and developed a style called "jazz poetry."

(4)   Hughes attended Lincoln University in Pennsylvania. Thurgood Marshall, the first African-American Supreme Court justice, was a classmate of his.

(5)   Langston Hughes worked as a crewman on a ship in 1923 during which time he visited South Africa, and Europe. He lived for a brief period in England in 1924.

(6)   On returning to the US, Hughes settled in Harlem, NY, where he lived for the remainder of his life.

(7)   Hughes wrote poetry, novels, and plays. He was active in the African-American literary society, helping to establish theatre projects in New York City and Chicago.

(8)   Hughes attempted to inspire pride in black people of lower socio-economic status, rather than insist that they aspire to a higher status.

Quotes from Langston Hughes

Hold fast to dreams, for if dreams die, life is a broken-winged bird that cannot fly.

Like a welcome summer rain, humor may suddenly cleanse and cool the earth, the air and you.

An artist must be free to choose what he does, certainly, but he must also never be afraid to do what he might choose.

When people care for you and cry for you, they can straighten out your soul

CHAPTER 13

THE GREAT DEPRESSION AND WORLD WAR II, 1929-1945

The Great Depression began with a US stock market collapse in October 1929. Throughout the 1930s the official unemployment rate in the United States was about 25%. (One out of every 4 workers could not find a job.) Those fortunate enough to have a job might be underemployed or employed only part-time. Many people gave up looking for work and were then no longer counted as unemployed. So it is safe to assume that a more realistic tabulation of unemployment would have been closer to 50%. The Depression was a worldwide phenomenon.

John Steinbeck (1902-1968) and *The Grapes of Wrath*

(1) John Steinbeck published 27 books; one, *The Grapes of Wrath*, the definitive, classic novel about life during the Great Depression, won the Pulitzer Prize.

(2) Other famous novels by Steinbeck include *East of Eden, Tortilla Flats, Canary Row,* and *Of Mice and Men.*

(3) Steinbeck was awarded the Nobel Prize for Literature in 1962.

(4) John Steinbeck attended Stanford University to study literature but did not graduate.

(5) After leaving Stanford, Steinbeck went to New York to pursue a career as a writer, but he failed to find a publisher at that time and returned to California.

(6) After a business venture failed for Steinbeck, his father provided housing for him and supported him and his wife as he attempted writing in California.

(7) As a World War II newspaper correspondent, Steinbeck actually took part in some of the battles, at one point manning a machine gun in an operation which took German prisoners. He also suffered shrapnel wounds from combat activities in the war.

(8) Steinbeck's death at age 66 was from heart disease, believed to have been advanced because of smoking.

Quotes from John Steinbeck

I have come to believe that a great teacher is a great artist and that there are as few as there are any other great artists. Teaching might even be the greatest of the arts since the medium is the human mind and spirit.

A journey is a person in itself; no two are alike. And all plans, safeguards, policing, and coercion are fruitless. We find that after years of struggle that we do not take a trip; a trip takes us.

Ideas are like rabbits. You get a couple and learn how to handle them, and pretty soon you have a dozen.

No one wants advice - only corroboration.[62]

No man really knows about other human beings. The best he can do is to suppose that they are like himself.

Will Rogers (1879-1935), Laughter and Wisdom

(1) Will Rogers is most famous as a humorist, whose wisdom and humanity inspired American during the Great Depression.

(2) Will Rogers was about one-quarter Cherokee, born in Oklahoma, the youngest of eight children. His father was a Confederate

---

[62] Corroboration: proof confirming the truth of a theory or idea.

Civil War veteran and a leader among the Cherokee tribe. "My ancestors didn't come over on the Mayflower, but they met the boat," said Will.

(3)   Rogers dropped out of school in the 10th grade and went to South Africa with a "wild west show."

(4)   Rogers had amazing skill with a rope and was famous for his rope tricks.

(5)   Rogers was an excellent horseman and polo player.

(6)   Rogers first became a star of vaudeville—telling jokes and doing rope tricks. From this he became a silent movie star.

(7)   Rogers was among the few silent movie starts who transitioned easily into sound movies ("talkies").

(8)   Rogers had a diverse entertainment career. He became a radio star, and he wrote a popular syndicated newspaper column. Rogers' humor in his radio show and newspaper column raised spirits during the Depression.

(9)   Roger, an aviation enthusiast, died in a plane crash in Alaska in 1935. The whole country was shocked and saddened by his passing. He is widely believed to have been the most popular man in America at that time.

Quotes from Will Rogers

Be thankful we're not getting all the government we're paying for.

Everything is funny, as long as it's happening to somebody else.

Even if you're on the right track, you'll get run over if you just sit there.

You've got to go out on a limb sometimes because that's where the fruit is.

The worst thing that happens to you may be the best thing for you if you don't let it get the best of you.

We will never have true civilization until we have learned to recognize the rights of others.

Good judgment comes from experience, and a lot of that comes from bad judgment.

Too many people spend money they haven't earned to buy things they don't want to impress people they don't like.

If you want to be successful, it's just this simple. Know what you are doing. Love what you are doing. And believe in what you are doing.

It isn't what we don't know that gives us trouble, it's what we know that ain't so.

Everybody is ignorant, only on different subjects.

Worrying is like paying on a debt that may never come due.

What the country needs is dirtier fingernails and cleaner minds.

Franklin D. Roosevelt (1882-1945) and the New Deal, US President 1933-1945

(1)   Franklin D. Roosevelt is considered to have been one of only three truly great American Presidents (along with Washington and Lincoln).

(2)   Franklin D. Roosevelt was born to a wealthy upstate New York family. He was a distant cousin of Theodore Roosevelt.

(3)   Franklin D. Roosevelt is well known by his initials FDR.

(4)   Franklin was educated at a private boarding school, then Harvard University.

(5)   Franklin Roosevelt married his distant cousin Eleanor Roosevelt in New York City on Saint Patrick's Day, 1905. President Theodore Roosevelt, Eleanor's uncle, gave away the bride. Franklin and Eleanor would have six children.

(6)   Franklin Roosevelt served two terms in the New York State legislature. In 1913 he was appointed Assistant Secretary of the

Navy under President Woodrow Wilson. Then in 1920 he was the Democratic candidate for Vice-President.

(7) In 1918 Franklin Roosevelt contracted and survived the Spanish flu which killed 20 million people world-wide.

(8) In 1921 Franklin Roosevelt's life changed dramatically. He contracted polio and became paralyzed from the waist down for the rest of his life. He fell into a severe depression while adjusting to his new life, and he considered permanent retirement from public life.

(9) Roosevelt returned to politics at the Democratic National Conventions of 1924 and 1928 with his vocal support of Al Smith for US President. Smith in turn encouraged Roosevelt to run for New York Governor in 1928. Roosevelt narrowly won that election. As he entered the governor's office in Albany, New York, Franklin Roosevelt's career had now encompassed three of the positions held by his famous cousin, Theodore—New York legislator, Assistant Secretary of the Navy, and New York Governor. And, like Theodore, he had also been the nominee of a major political party for Vice-President.

(10) Roosevelt developed the art of appearing to be able to walk. With the help of leg braces which locked in place, Roosevelt appeared to be able to stand. Then by holding firmly to the arm of his son and vigorously throwing a shoulder forward, he could appear to walk a few steps. In reality Roosevelt could not move his legs at all and could not stand without the braces holding him up. But at the time, American's would not have accepted that their President was "a cripple." Few people really knew the extent of Roosevelt's disability.

(11) The stock market crash of 1929 began the Great Depression of the 1930s. Republican President Herbert Hoover was unable to turn around the economy and was perceived as reluctant to take action to help the poor. All over the country people lost their jobs and became homeless. In many places the homeless set up makeshift camps of cardboard and scrap houses which became known as "Hoovervilles." The crisis led to the defeat of Hoover in his bid for reelection. The new President elected in 1932 was Franklin D. Roosevelt.

(12) Roosevelt's campaign song had been "Happy Days Are Here Again" and Will Rogers had been one of his most enthusiastic proponents. During his inauguration speech Roosevelt proclaimed "We have nothing to fear but fear itself." The mood of the country was suddenly uplifted.

(13) The 1932 election had been a Democratic landslide.[63] With large Democratic majorities in both Houses of Congress and a feeling of urgency hanging over the country, Roosevelt set about proposing legislation. His first 100 days in office produced more legislation (passed and signed into law) than any other 100 days before or since. As a result, every new president since Franklin Roosevelt has his first 100 days in office compared to "the 100 days" in 1933.

(14) Roosevelt called his administration and policies "the New Deal." The basis of the New Deal was pragmatism, not idealism.[64] Roosevelt saw that the times demanded results.

(15) Historians classify the Roosevelt policies as "relief," "recovery," or "reform" based on their intent. Most of the policies of the 100 days were relief polices. They were designed to provide immediate help for the poor and unemployed. The best known, most popular, and probably the most successful relief program was the Civilian Conservation Corps (CCC). The CCC program is credited by those who participated as "life changing."

(16) Roosevelt put forward two major recovery programs: the National Recovery Act (NRA), designed to help businesses, and the Agricultural Adjustment Act (AAA) to help farmers. Both were eventually judged unconstitutional by the Supreme Court.

(17) Roosevelt's reform policies were designed to establish long-tern change. They included Social Security Insurance, the Federal Deposit Insurance Corporation (FDIC), the Rural Electrification Act (REA), and the Tennessee Valley Authority (TVA).

---

[63] "Landslide" (in politics): An election in which one side wins by a wide margin.

[64] Pragmatism: concentration of efforts on getting results, rather than the methods or principles involved in achieving those results.

(18) FDR gave a series of informal speeches, "Fireside Chats", from the White House on the radio to reassure the American people. These were very popular.

(19) Roosevelt was reelected in 1936, then again in 1940 and in 1944. He was elected four times and died in office in 1945. After his death a constitutional amendment was passed, limiting the President to two terms.

(20) Roosevelt's policies did improve people's lives, but they did not end the Great Depression. The Depression did not really end until World War II forced governments to engage in massive deficit spending.

(21) For political reasons, Roosevelt did not want to be photographed in his wheelchair. Amazingly, the press of his time respected the President's wishes. Thousands of photos were taken of Roosevelt while he was President, but only two of those show him in a wheelchair.

(22) After the Supreme Court had struck down Roosevelt's two big recovery programs as unconstitutional, Roosevelt asked Congress for the authority to expand the Court to 15 members so that he could appoint six new justices who would tend to vote his way. Congress rejected the proposal as an attempt to weaken the Supreme Court and concentrate too much power in the President—a "Court Packing" scheme.

(23) World War II in Europe began in September 1939 when Germany (and the USSR) attacked Poland. In Asia, Japan had already been actively aggressive in China for years.

(24) France was quickly knock out of the war and Britain was left standing alone against Nazi Germany. Roosevelt and the US Congress favored Britain and offered "Lend-lease Aid" to provide needed supplies, but the US officially remained neutral through 1940 and nearly all of 1941.

(25) The US entered World War II on December 7, 1941 when the Japanese made a surprise attack on Pearl Harbor, Hawaii. The next day the US declared war on Japan, and Germany declared war on the US in support of her ally, Japan.

(26) As the US was entering the war, Roosevelt and Churchill agreed to concentrate on defeating Germany first, believing it to be the greater threat. While the concentration was on Germany, the US made steady progress in defeating Japan after the decisive Battle of Midway in June 1942, during which four Japanese aircraft carriers were sunk.

(27) American engagement in the war against Nazi Germany began with a landing and campaign in North Africa. Hard won success there eventually allowed for a landing in Sicily, followed by landing in Italy and the Italian campaign. But all these campaigns were slow and did little in challenge the power of Nazi Germany.

(28) The combined US-British landing in Normandy, France on June 6, 1944 was the most outstanding military accomplishment of the 20th century. The landing was necessary in order to place the armies in position to threaten the heartland of Germany. The war's end in Europe came with the capture of Berlin 11 months after the landing. Japan would be brought to surrender a few months after Germany by the use of nuclear weapons—the only two atom bombs ever used up to now.

(29) As the war appeared to be nearly won, Congress became concerned with how the US economy would absorb a large number of newly discharged soldiers into the job market. To reduce the sudden shock, Congress passed the GI Bill of Rights, which included generous benefits to allow veterans to attend college. After the war, a large numbers of veterans used the GI Bill to get an education. The much greater number of educated people (nearly all men) caused an economic boom, creating long-term changes in the American economy and greater social mobility.

(30) Roosevelt did not live to see the end of the war. He suffered a fatal stroke in April 1945, just one month before the German surrender. The reaction to Roosevelt's death was a huge outpouring of grief.

(31) When the Franklin Roosevelt Statue in Washington, DC was being planned, an argument developed between those who wanted to show Roosevelt in his wheelchair and those who did not. On the one hand, Roosevelt in his wheelchair could be

inspiring for the disabled and their advocates. On the other hand, Roosevelt, himself, never wanted photos taken of him in the wheelchair, and he never appeared in public in the wheelchair. The final design shows FDR with a cloak draped over his chair concealing the base and his dog Fala at his feet.

(32) In 1938 Franklin Roosevelt founded the March of Dimes, a charity which encouraged children to collect dimes to finance research to find a cure for polio, the disease which had caused his paralysis. Effective polio vaccines resulted from this. The March of Dimes still exists, now focusing on complications of birth. FDR's was honored in 1945, shortly after his death, with his image on the dime.

Quotes from Franklin D. Roosevelt

Happiness lies in the joy of achievement and the thrill of creative effort.

We have always held to the hope, the belief, the conviction that there is a better life, a better world, beyond the horizon.

There are many ways of going forward, but only one way of standing still.

It is common sense to take a method and try it. If it fails, admit it frankly and try another. But above all, try something.

The only limit to our realization of tomorrow will be our doubts of today.

Men are not prisoners of fate, but only prisoners of their own minds.

I'm not the smartest fellow in the world, but I can sure pick smart colleagues.

The virtues are lost in self-interest as rivers are lost in the sea.

Remember you are just an extra in everyone else's play.

(Anna) Eleanor Roosevelt (1884-1962), First Lady of the World

(1) Anna Eleanor Roosevelt is the undisputed greatest American First Lady.

(2) Eleanor Roosevelt is also often called "the First Lady of the World." Her long career in American politics and world affairs extended, and her role even increased, after Franklin's death.

(3) Eleanor Roosevelt was the niece of President Theodore Roosevelt. She was also a distant cousin of her husband Franklin Roosevelt.

(4) Eleanor's father (Theodore's brother) died when Eleanor was still quite young.

(5) Eleanor was self-conscious of her looks. As a child she often heard her mother speak of her as "plain" (not pretty).

(6) When Franklin Roosevelt contracted polio, Eleanor changed her life to meet the challenge. She became active in the New York Democratic Party to keep Franklin's name alive while encouraging him to reconnect and stay active in politics. She did new things which had frightened her before. She learned to drive a car. Before the polio, Eleanor had been content to sit quietly in the background. Eleanor was also forced to confront Franklin Roosevelt's dominating mother who wanted FDR to simply retire when he became disabled.

(7) Eleanor shared Franklin's concern for the poor and desire to build a more just society, and she felt less confined by political realities than he did. For her role as First Lady, she can be considered "the conscience of the New Deal."

(8) Eleanor was also "the legs of the New Deal." Franklin's Roosevelt's physical disability made travel difficult. Eleanor went all over the country to represent her husband.

(9) Eleanor Roosevelt disliked formal social events and what she called "small talk", and she confided to friends that she at first dreaded becoming First Lady. Her actions and activities redefined the role of First Lady.

(10) As First Lady, Eleanor wrote a daily syndicated newspaper column called "My Day."

(11) Eleanor Roosevelt was the first First Lady to hold her own news conference. She was also the first First Lady to speak at a National Convention of a major political party.

(12) As First Lady, Eleanor Roosevelt often commented on controversial social and political issues, such as racial discrimination in the South, which President Roosevelt avoided for political reasons. When reporters then asked the President about Eleanor's outspoken statements, FDR would say "I can't control what my Misses says."

(13) In 1939 the Daughters of the American Revolution denied an African-American opera singer, Marion Anderson, the use of Constitutional Hall for a concert because of her race. Eleanor Roosevelt then promptly resigned her membership in the Daughters of the American Revolution and arranged for Ms. Anderson to perform at an outdoor concert at the Lincoln Memorial.

(14) World War II ended one month after the death of Franklin Roosevelt. The new US President Harry Truman asked Eleanor Roosevelt to represent the US on the Committee for Human Rights in the new United Nations. She became the Chairperson of that committee and they wrote the Universal Declaration of Human Rights, which remains as one of the most important documents in use in the United Nations today.

(15) President Truman called Eleanor Roosevelt "the First Lady of the World" in tribute to her achievement with the Human Rights Committee.

(16) Eleanor Roosevelt continued to be active in Democratic Party politics until her death in 1962. She became a kind of godmother of the party, and her endorsement was sought by Democratic Party presidential candidates.

(17) During the Presidential Administration of John F. Kennedy, Eleanor Roosevelt chaired the President's Commission on the Status of Women.

Quotes from Eleanor Roosevelt

With the new day comes new strength and new thoughts.

Great minds discuss ideas; average minds discuss events; small minds discuss people.

A woman is like a tea bag - you can't tell how strong she is until you put her in hot water.

You gain strength, courage, and confidence by every experience in which you really stop to look fear in the face...you must do the thing that you think you cannot do.

The future belongs to those who believe in the beauty of their dreams.

You have to accept whatever comes and the only important thing is that you meet it with courage and with the best that you have to give.

No one can make you feel inferior without your consent.

It is better to light a candle than curse the darkness.

Happiness is not a goal; it is a by-product.

Remember always that you not only have the right to be an individual, you have an obligation to be one.

It is not more vacation we need - it is more vocation.

Mary McLeod Bethune (1875-1955) and FDR's Black Cabinet

(1) Around 1938 Mary Jane Bethune met Eleanor Roosevelt in the course of their political work. The two women became close friends and Bethune became a central figure in the Federal Council of Negro Affairs, informally known as Roosevelt's "Black Cabinet." This group advised Roosevelt on issues of concern to African-Americans.

(2) Mary McLeod was born in South Carolina in 1875 into a large, impoverished, rural family. Her parents were former slaves, and she was one of their 17 children.

(3) Mary attended a one room school house for African-American children run by Presbyterian missionaries. She was the only child in the family to attend school.

(4) Mary McLeod received her higher education through a scholarship which her primary teacher helped to arrange.

(5) Mary McLeod hoped to serve as a missionary in Africa, but ironically she was denied this because of her race. She began her teaching career at a missionary school in Augusta, Georgia.

(6) Mary married Albert Bethune in 1898 and the couple moved to Florida the following year. There Mary ran her own school for girls, emphasizing character and practical skills. Albert left the family in 1907.

(7) Mary McLeod Bethune started her school on a shoe string budget, then worked hard at fund raising to support her school, and it continued to grow. A large donation from John D. Rockefeller helped the expansion.

(8) In 1931 with the help from the Methodist Church, Bethune merged her girls' school with a successful boys' school. The new school became a junior college and Bethune became the college president. A few year later, this institution, Bethune-Cookman School, became a four year college.

(9) Bethune served as the president of the Florida chapter of the National Association of Colored Women from 1917 until 1925.

(10) Bethune served as president of the National Association of Colored Women in 1924 and helped the organization establish a permanent headquarters in Washington, DC. She was also elected president of the Southern Association of Colored Women's Clubs in 1920. The goals of these clubs were empowerment of black women, especially through voter registration.

Quotes from Mary McLeod Bethune

Faith is the first factor in a life devoted to service. Without it, nothing is possible. With it, nothing is impossible.

Invest in the human soul. Who knows, it might be a diamond in the rough.

The whole world opened to me when I learned to read.

World War II and America's "Greatest Generation"

A book by the journalist, Tom Brokaw, labeled the Americans who participated in World War II as the "greatest generation." They were. From December 1941 to 1945, the entire American society came together with one singular purpose—to defeat evil. And they defeated it. Many minority groups, which at that time did not enjoy equal right and equal opportunity we all enjoy today, still sacrifice for the greater good. Mexican-Americans, Native-Americans, and African-Americans all enlisted in the military in great numbers, while millions of women went to work in factories doing jobs no one thought they could before. The African-American "Tuskegee Airmen" distinguished themselves as the best fighter pilots in the Army Air Corps. The Native-American Navajo Code Talkers saved the lives of fellow Marines by their rapid and near perfect transmission of radio messages in combat. And the Nisei Japanese-American 442nd Infantry Regiment proved their loyalty with great courage and devotion to duty while many of their kin waited out the war in internment camps. Fighting men in all the services focused on duty, not self.

Daniel Inouye (1924-2012) and the Nisei Warriors

(1) Daniel Inouye was born in Honolulu, Hawaii to Japanese-American parents. During World War II when west coast Japanese-Americans were locked into internment camps, those in Hawaii were not interned.

(2) Inouye volunteered for serving in the army in 1943 and was assigned to the 442nd Regimental Combat Team. This was the all Japanese-American unit which fought in Europe. The 442nd (Nisei) distinguished itself as the most decorated unit of its size in all American history. About 14,000 men total served in the unit over a two year period, earning more than 9,000 Purple Hearts and 21 Congressional Medals of Honor—all this while members of west coast Japanese-American families were locked up in internment camps for fear that they might be spies or saboteurs.[65]

(3) During one battle Daniel Inouye was struck in the chest, but the bullet was stopped by two silver dollars he was carrying in his shirt.

(4) Daniel Inouye lost his right arm and won the Purple Heart and Congressional Medal of Honor in a battle in Italy on April 21, 1945 (about two weeks before the end of the war in Europe). He had already been wounded in the stomach in that battle but continued to attack a machine gun nest even after his arm was mutilated by a rifle grenade. He threw his last grenade with his left hand and sustained another wound—that one to the leg—before he passed out.

(5) Inouye had to abandon his dream of becoming a surgeon because of the loss of the arm. He attended law school instead.

(6) Inouye served as Hawaii's first regular member of the House of Representative when the territory became a state.

(7) Inouye was elected to the Senate in 1962 and served fifty years in the Senate until his death in 2012. He rose to the rank of President Pro Tempore of the Senate, making him third in the line of Presidential succession.

---

[65] Purple Heart: the medal given to servicemen wounded in combat.
Congressional Medal of Honor: the highest military award for distinguish bravery in battle.

Quotes from Daniel Inouye

Americanism is not a matter of skin or color.

I hope that the mistakes made and suffering imposed upon Japanese-Americans nearly 60 years ago will not be repeated against Arab-Americans whose loyalties are now being called into question.

My first thought was that I could no longer play the ukulele, and my dream of becoming a surgeon was over. But it's a funny thing — I never considered myself a cripple or an invalid. It just never became part of my thinking. It isn't part of my thinking today.

PART 4

POST WORLD WAR II AND THE EMERGENCE OF THE MODERN ERA

I n 1945 at the conclusion of World War II, the United States had defeated the joint evils of Nazism, fascism, and military imperialism. But this had not been accomplished alone. The Soviet Union (Russia) could rightly claim that it had fought longer and sacrificed more against larger Nazi forces than had the US and Britain combined. In the process of that fight, the Soviet Union had conquered most of Eastern Europe, and Soviet leader, Joseph Stalin intended to continue to keep control Eastern Europe.

The Soviets and the Americans soon came to view each other as mortal enemies. This led leaders in both countries to view world politics and world conflict narrowly through the lens of the US-Soviet rivalry. This oversimplification caused both sides to live in perpetual fear and to make catastrophic blunders.

A "Cold War" evolved in which both sides tried to manipulate world affairs to gain allies. China also figured into the mix, as communists and non-communists continued to struggle against each other until the communist victory in 1949. After the Soviet Union developed nuclear weapons, both sides blustered but stopped short of direct conflict. The state of the US-Soviet conflict of that time has been described as a stalemate with both sides prevented from actual war by a "MAD" condition (Mutually Assured Destruction). "Proxy wars" were fought in countries such as

Greece, Cuba, Korea, and Vietnam.[66] By the middle 1970s an uneasy "détente" developed in which the US and the Soviet Union accepted the undeniable reality that the other would continue to exist.

The other major theme of the post-war era is the struggle for civil rights in the United States. By 1945 African-Americans had come to a juncture where most agreed that little progress had been made in race relations and equality would never be achieved without radical action. Two camps evolved as to what form that radical action might take—violence or nonviolence.

---

[66] Proxy: a substitute used to stand in for the real thing.

CHAPTER 14

COLD WAR—PART I, 1945-1963

Harry S. Truman (1884-1972), the Fair Deal and the Truman Doctrine, US President 1945-1953

(1)   Harry Truman was born to a farm family in Missouri. He was the only President in the twentieth century to not have attended college (university), but he was also believed to have read nearly every book in his hometown library as a child.

(2)   Harry Truman served as an artillery officer during World War I.

(3)   Harry Truman's career as a politician was promoted by his association with Thomas Pendergast, boss of the Kansas City Democratic political machine. Pendergast had so much control of politics in the KC region that when Truman was elected to the Senate he was sometimes disparagingly referred to as "the Senator from Pendergast" by his colleagues.

(4)   Truman had been Vice-President for only three months when Franklin Roosevelt suddenly died leaving Truman to be President. Truman had big shoes to fill and few people thought that anyone could fill the shoes of FDR. Upon FDR's death, Harry Truman graciously comforted Eleanor Roosevelt and asked if he could do anything to help her to which Mrs. Roosevelt jokingly replied that he should ask her for help because, she said "You're the one in trouble now."

(5)   President Truman's political associate and friend, Tom Pendergast, had been convicted of crimes involving political

corruption and served 15 months in prison, after which he was penniless and abandoned by his wife and most of his friends. He died in 1945 and Harry Truman, who had only recently been sworn in as President insisted on attending the funeral. This created a minor scandal.

(6) The war in Europe was concluded just one month after Truman became President. But the war with Japan did not appear to be near conclusion.

(7) Franklin Roosevelt failed to inform Vice-President Truman about the Manhattan Project to build the atomic bomb. So, on taking office as President, Harry Truman did not know about the bomb.

(8) President Truman made the decision to use the atomic bomb on Japan. Two atomic bombs were dropped. The first was on Hiroshima on August 6, 1945. Because Japan did not surrender immediately, a second atomic bomb was dropped on Nagasaki three days later. The two atomic bombs dropped on Japan are still the only atomic bombs ever used in all human history. Today we might say that Truman's decision to use these was inhuman, but the decision at that time was more complicated. Truman's military advisors informed him that the only way Japan would surrender would be through invasion and conquest of the Japanese mainland, and they estimated that this would cost the lives of a half million or more American soldiers.

(9) The United States and the Soviet Union (Russia) emerged from World War II as the two great superpowers. The Soviet Union had actually contributed and sacrificed much more in the ground war against Nazi Germany. And at the conclusion of the war, the Soviet Union had by far the largest and most powerful land army in the world.

(10) The United States and the Soviet Union had competing ideologies. The US was democratic and capitalist. The Soviet Union was authoritarian and communist. Each felt threatened by the other, and each looked to dominate the world with its particular ideology.

(11) The Soviet Union installed "puppet governments" in the Eastern European countries which it had occupied during the war.[67] Then the Soviet Union attempted to expand its influence by supporting communist revolutions in other countries. In 1947 President Truman got a large appropriation from Congress to support the governments of Greece and Turkey against communist insurgents.[68] At that time he announced "the Truman Doctrine," that the US would support any government resisting communist aggression.

(12) As the successor to FDR's "New Deal," Harry Truman dubbed his administration the "Fair Deal."

(13) President Truman was not expected to win reelection in 1948. His Democratic Party had fractured. Southern Democrats were unhappy because Truman had issued an executive order integrating the army, and Progressive Democrats did not think Truman was progressive enough. The Southern Democrats called themselves "Dixiecrats" and nominated their own candidate. Progressive Democrats also nominated their candidate. With the Democratic Party split three ways, the polls showed that the Republican candidate had a big lead and was certain to win. Early in the evening, election results showed the Republican with such a big lead that the *Chicago Tribune* printed the headline "Dewey Defeats Truman" for its Wednesday morning edition. But when the final results were in, Truman had been reelected. Many of today's textbooks display the famous photo of President Truman with a big smile as he holds up the Chicago paper.

(14) The United States and its Western European allies formed NATO (the North Atlantic Treaty Organization) in 1949 for the purpose of resisting potential Soviet (Russian) aggression with the central tenant that any attack on one NATO member would be considered an attack on all members.

(15) President Truman's most successful anti-Communist policy was the Marshall Plan (named after Secretary of State George Marshall). Through the Marshall Plan, the US financed the

---

[67] Puppet government: a government control by another country.
[68] Insurgent: a person who revolts against the government.

rebuilding of Europe from the war damage of World War II. Because of the Marshall Plan, Western Europe rebuilt rapidly, became prosperous, and the countries of Western Europe became important trade partners and allies of the US.

(16) After World War II, Germany had been carved into four zones of occupation (American, Soviet, British, and French). The three western zones were soon unified into the country of West Germany while the eastern, Soviet zone, became East Germany. Occupation and geopolitics were complicated because the four zone solution used for occupation of Germany was also used for the occupation of the German capital city, Berlin. The problem was that all of Berlin was within East Germany. The allies (the US, the UK, and France) refused to give up Berlin to the Soviet communists. Together they set up the city of West Berlin. West Berlin was in theory a part of West Germany, but it was located near the center of East Germany. As a capitalist city and an ally of the US and Western Europe and a beneficiary of the Marshall Plan, West Berlin was prosperous and free while East Berlin was impoverished and totalitarian. This became a big problem for the Soviet communist government of East Germany, because people with talent and prospects would flee from East Germany to West Berlin where they could escape to West Germany. In 1948 East Germany and the Soviet Union decided to solve their problem by starving out West Berlin. They closed all access to West Berlin. The Truman administration countered with the "Berlin Airlift." For a year there were constant, around the clock flights bringing food and supplies into Berlin. The pilots had to fly very specific routes at high altitude to avoid being shot down. Eventually the Soviets conceded that their blockade was unsuccessful and not worth the cost to continue.

(17) The House (of Representatives) Un-American Activities Committee wielded unprecedented power for a time and called in hundreds of people whom they were investigating for communist ties. Many who refused to cooperate were jailed for contempt of Congress. In another curious sign of the times, most employment applications at that time and for years to come asked

the question "Are you now, or have you ever been, a member of the Communist Party?" Why should McDonald's want to know this if I am applying to fry burgers?

What was going on? During the long Great Depression, many people were looking for answers. Some joined the American Communist Party, which grew large, and many attended Communist Party meetings. These activities were not illegal, as a matter of fact, the Constitution specifically grants people the right to assemble, speak freely, and protest. The Communist Party was, however, a threat because the Soviet (Russian) Communists encouraged violent overthrown of the government.

People called before the House Un-American Activities were party members, those who had attended even one meeting, and those who associated with Party members. When testifying before the House Committee, those accused were pressured to name others who might have attended a meeting. Those who were called to testify were sometime fired from their jobs and often had difficulty finding new work. This was especially true in government and in the entertainment industry. Many careers were ruined.

(18) At the conclusion of World War II, the country of Korea was divided for the purpose of occupation into Soviet communist north and the American protectorate south. This situation evolved into a permanent separation between the countries of North Korea and South Korea. In 1950 North Korea attacked South Korea. The United Nations Security Council voted to send troops to help South Korea. War was never declared. Officially this was a "police action" by the United Nations. Many countries provided troops, but over 90% of the United Nations forces were troops from the United States and the mission was under US leadership. This police action dragged on for three years and cost many American lives. As a result of his inability to bring the Korean War (police action) to a conclusion, President Truman was unpopular at the time he left office in January 1953.

(19) President Truman relieved Five Star General Douglas MacArthur of command in Korean for attempting to expand the Korean War to a full scale war with China. MacArthur had been manipulating behind the President's back to gain support for the expansion in Congress and in Europe. The removal of the popular general, which was probably necessary, hurt President Truman's already flagging reputation.

Quotes from Harry S. Truman

It is amazing what you can accomplish if you do not care who gets the credit.

A pessimist is one who makes difficulties of his opportunities and an optimist is one who makes opportunities of his difficulties.

If you can't stand the heat, get out of the kitchen.

Dwight "Ike" D. Eisenhower (1890-1969), Brinkmanship and the Military-Industrial Complex, US President 1953-1961

(1) Dwight D. Eisenhower was born and raised in Kansas. His family was not well off, and he occasionally got into fights with boys who made fun of his hand-me-down clothes. He played high school football and baseball. He chose to attend the US Military Academy at West Point partly because they had a good football program.

(2) During his boyhood, a simple knee scrape caused an infection which threatened Dwight Eisenhower's life and kept him out of school for most of a year. The doctor treating him was considering amputation.

(3) Dwight Eisenhower was a running back and linebacker on the West Point football team until a knee injury ended his career.

(4) Dwight Eisenhower actually played against Jim's Thorpe's Carlisle Indian School in 1912. Thorp had won Gold Medals in

the pentathlon and decathlon in Olympics in Sweden just months before, and the Swedish king had famously called Thorpe the greatest athlete in the world. Carlisle won that game against Army 27-6, and Thorpe had a 97 yard kickoff return.

(5) Dwight Eisenhower spent many years in the shadow of General Douglas MacArthur, as MacArthur's top assistant with the rank of major.

(6) Eisenhower was not promoted to brigadier general (one star general) until September 1941, but he rose quickly to four star rank during World War II.

(7) Lieutenant General Eisenhower (3 stars) commanded the allied invasion of North Africa in 1942.

(8) General Eisenhower, now with four stars, commanded D-Day, the allied invasion of France on June 6, 1944 against strongly fortified German forces. The success of the D-Day landing was the greatest allied achievement of World War II.

(9) Eisenhower remained as Supreme Allied Commander on the Western Front in Europe from D-Day until the end of the war. In December 1944 he was promoted to General of the Army (5 stars), the highest possible rank in the entire military structure.

(10) After the war, Eisenhower retired from active military service briefly, during which time he served as President of Columbia University. He returned to active service to become Commander of NATO forces in Europe.

(11) Eisenhower published his World War II memoirs, entitled *Crusade for Europe*. Other books which he published later include *At Easy: Stories I Tell to my Friends*; *Mandate for Change*; *The Eisenhower Diaries*; and *Letters to Mamie*.

(12) Because of his status as America's greatest war hero, both major parties attempted to convince Eisenhower to accept their nominations for US President. He decided to run as a Republican in 1952.

(13) During the 1952 campaign, the Korean War was in its third year. Ike pledged that, if elected, he would go to Korea, and he would bring about an end to the war. He fulfilled his promise to go to Korea as President-elect, and a negotiated settlement of the war was arranged in July 1953.

(14) Dwight Eisenhower served two full terms as President, despite experiencing a heart attack during his first term. The country remained generally prosperous during his tenure in office, and he left office as a very popular President.

(15) Eisenhower was the first US President to hold a televised press conference.

(16) President Eisenhower's Cold War policies centered on what he called "brinkmanship". He said that the US would go to the brink of war to stop communist aggression. He also talked of "roll back", the hope that aggressive American action could roll back gains made by communists in recent years.

(17) It was during Eisenhower's time that the CIA accelerated its attempts to manipulate governments and politics in other countries. The worst example from this time is in Guatemala. The CIA was also involved in Cuba. Fidel Castro seized power in Cuba in 1959, and the CIA immediately began training anti-Castro insurgents from Cuba at a base in Florida. The US also began its involvement in Vietnam under Eisenhower and backed the tyrannical rule of the Shaw of Iran.

(18) A problem which had begun under President Truman was perpetuated under President Eisenhower. US Cold War foreign policies were being made based on what we were against (communism) rather than what we said we were for (democracy).

(19) In 1957 the Soviet Union launched *Sputnik*, the first satellite to orbit the earth. This caused President Eisenhower to fear that the Soviet Union was surpassing the US in science and technology and this could pose a serious threat to national security. The President's response was to propose much greater federal support for education, especially in the sciences. President Eisenhower's education policies are now considered to have been among his greatest achievements.

(20) US fear of communism during the Cold War period seems today to have bordered on paranoia.[69] To understand it, we must remember that Soviet Communism under Joseph Stalin was horribly brutal and inhumane, and this was the style of

---

[69] Paranoia: extreme, irrational fear.

government that the Soviet Union seemed to want to export to the entire world. The US experienced what has been called the "Second Red Scare" which lasted through the 1950s and well into the 1960s.

(21) During his first term, President Eisenhower was harassed by Wisconsin Senator Joseph McCarthy, who accused the President of employed communist sympathizers in the State Department. Eisenhower was reluctant to answer McCarty's accusations, saying that he would not "get down in the gutter" with the Senator. McCarthy was eventually discredited and censured[70] by the Senate.

(22) President Eisenhower took a special interest in improving the nation's highway system. Many of today's interstate highways were constructed during the Eisenhower years.

(23) Eisenhower's campaign slogan, "I like Ike" became a popular expression in the United States during his time in office.

(24) In May 1960 Soviet Premier Nikita Khrushchev accused the Eisenhower administration of sending spy planes over the Soviet Union. President Eisenhower at first denied the claim, but was forced to admit it was true, when the Soviets produced a captures pilot from a downed aircraft.

(25) Eisenhower was a fiscal conservative. He thought that excessive government spending could be a serious threat to national security. He limited government spending and shocked Americans by reducing military spending. In his farewell address he warned that the "military-industrial complex" was a leading threat to American security.

Quotes from Dwight D. Eisenhower

The supreme quality for leadership is unquestionably integrity.

Whatever America hopes to bring to pass in the world must first come to pass in the hearts of America.

---

[70] Censured: condemned. "Senate censure" meant that McCarthy would not be allowed to return to the Senate chamber.

Neither a wise man nor a brave man lies down on the tracks of history to wait for the train of the future to run over him.

Motivation is the art of getting people to do what you want them to do because they want to do it.

I hate war as only a soldier who has lived it can, only as one who has seen its brutality, its futility, its stupidity.

Every gun that is made, every warship launched, every rocket fired, signifies in the final sense a theft from those who hunger and are not fed, those who are cold and are not clothed.

We must guard against the acquisition of unwarranted influence, whether sought or unsought, by the military-industrial complex.

Peace and justice are two sides of the same coin.

What counts is not necessarily the size of the dog in the fight - it's the size of the fight in the dog.

John F. Kennedy (1917-1963) and the New Frontier, US President 1961-1963

(1) John Kennedy was born to a wealthy Massachusetts family and educated at Harvard.

(2) Kennedy volunteered for the army at the beginning of World War II, but was rejected because of back problems. (His back problems continued to plague him his whole life.) After being rejected by the army, Kennedy then served as a naval officer.

(3) Kennedy became a war hero by saving several men who were on his patrol boat with him at the time that a Japanese torpedo sunk the boat.

(4) Kennedy won the Pulitzer Prize for literature for his book, *Profiles in Courage*.

(5) Kennedy served in the US Senate representing Massachusetts from 1953 to 1961.

(6) The tradition of televised debates between Presidential candidates began with the famous Kennedy-Nixon debates of 1960.

(7) Kennedy was elected President in 1960 at the age of 43. This made him the youngest man ever elected President. He was not, however, the youngest President. That was Theodore Roosevelt who had been elected Vice-president and took over the presidency when William McKinley was assassinated in 1901.

(8) Kennedy was the first (and as yet the only) Roman Catholic elected President. At the time this was a bigger deal than it would be today, because some people feared that a Catholic President would take orders from the Pope.

(9) Like FDR, Kennedy is also popularly known by his initials—JFK.

(10) John Kennedy called his administration the "New Frontier."

(11) On March 1, 1961 while still new in office, President Kennedy signed an executive order creating the Peace Corps.

(12) Relations between the US and Latin-America were not good when President Kennedy took office owing to alleged CIA meddling in the internal affairs of Latin-American countries. Kennedy launched "the Alliance for Progress" which provide aid to Latin-America. By the time of Kennedy's death, three years later, the image of the US among Latin-Americans had changed completely.

(13) Kennedy inherited a CIA plan for Cubans trained in Florida to invade Cuba and overthrow Fidel Castro. The plan was ill conceived and Kennedy vacillated in his support of it even while giving the okay for the attack.[71] The result was a disaster. Most of the invaders were killed or captured quickly, and Kennedy was criticized for having appeared to consent to air support then changed his mind at the last minute. This was the greatest embarrassment the Kennedy administration ever experienced. It happened just a few months after JFK had taken office. He went

---

[71] Vacillate: to incline first to an idea then switch back and forth to opposition.

on television taking full responsibility for the failure. The event is known in history for its location, "the Bay of Pigs."

(14) The Bay of Pigs incident may have embolden the Soviet Union. In 1962 the CIA discovered that the Soviets had placed offensive missiles in Cuba with nuclear capability. Kennedy demanded their immediate removal. This affair, "the Cuban Missile Crisis," led to a US blockade of Cuba. The Soviet Union backed down and removed the missiles.

(15) It was during the Kennedy administration that the Soviet Union constructed the Berlin Wall to stem the flood of talented East Germans using West Berlin as an escape route. Kennedy could do nothing to eliminate the wall, but he did go to Berlin and delivered a public speech strongly supporting West Berlin.

(16) President Kennedy negotiated the first nuclear arms limitation treaty between the US and the Soviet Union.

(17) Kennedy began America's serious involvement in Vietnam. President Eisenhower had committed the US to support that government with the SEATO Treaty (South-East Asian Treaty Organization). Kennedy was honoring the SEATO agreement, and he feared that a communist takeover in Vietnam could lead other countries in the region to fall to communism.[72] Under JFK, American military forces in Vietnam were small but growing, and they were beginning to be involved in direct combat operations. Kennedy was slow to see the signs of problems in Vietnam. By the beginning of 1963 the Vietnamese government was proving itself to be corrupt and unrepresentative of the will of the Vietnamese people. That summer a Buddhist monk burned himself alive in the center of Saigon to protest the people's anger with their government. The Vietnamese president, Ngo Dinh Diem, was overthrown and killed in November 1963 with the blessing of the CIA.

(18) President Kennedy was assassinated in Dallas, Texas in November 1963.

(19) John F. Kennedy's image is on the half dollar.

---

[72] The "domino theory" was the belief that countries would fall one after another to communism. This was a popular Cold War theory.

Quotes from John F. Kennedy

Ask not what your country can do for you; ask what you can do for your country.

As we express our gratitude, we must never forget that the highest appreciation is not to utter words, but to live by them.

Things do not happen. Things are made to happen.

Change is the law of life. And those who look only to the past or present are certain to miss the future.

Let us not seek the Republican answer or the Democratic answer, but the right answer. Let us not seek to fix the blame for the past. Let us accept our own responsibility for the future.

Efforts and courage are not enough without purpose and direction.

Those who dare to fail miserably can achieve greatly.

The time to repair the roof is when the sun is shining.

Those who make peaceful revolution impossible will make violent revolution inevitable.

The ignorance of one voter in a democracy impairs the security of all.

CHAPTER 15

THE MODERN CIVIL RIGHTS MOVEMENT, 1945-1970

Jackie Robinson (1919-1972), Integrating Major League Baseball

(1) In 1947 Jackie Robinson became the first African-American player in modern times to play for a major league baseball team.

(2) Jackie Robinson was born to a sharecropping family in Georgia in 1919.

(3) Jackie's father abandoned the family in 1920 and his mother then moved them to Southern California.

(4) Jackie Robinson was a star athlete in high school. He participated at a high level in football, basketball, baseball, track, and tennis. He was encouraged to participate in sports by an older brother who had won a silver medal in the 1936 Olympics.

(5) Robinson continued his impressive athletic career in multiple sports, first at Pasadena Community College, then at UCLA. He was a member of the 1939 undefeated UCLA football team. He was also the top scorer in the Pacific Coast Basketball Conference one year while playing for UCLA.

(6) Robinson left college without graduating and played some semi-professional football.

(7) Robinson was drafted into the army in 1942 (right after Pearl Harbor). He attended Officer Training School and was

commissioned as a second lieutenant. In 1944 he got into a confrontation with a bus driver when he was told to move to the back of the bus because of his race. The incident escalated when Robinson refused to back down. This led to a court martial (military trial). In that trial, Robinson was acquitted of insubordination. But the incident and trial kept Robinson from deploying to Europe with his unit. He was then discharged honorably in November.

(8) Robinson played shortstop for the Kansas City Monarchs of the Negro League in 1945, compiling an impressive batting average of .387.

(9) In 1946 Jackie Robinson was signed by General Manager Branch Rickey of the Brooklyn Dodgers after an extensive interview in which Rickey discussed the racial problem extensively with Robinson. Rickey insisted that he get a pledge from Robinson not to fight back against racial slurs, at least not for the first year. "I want a Negro player with guts enough not to fight back," said Rickey. Both men were aware that what they were about to do would be historic, Robinson would be insulted on a daily basis, and the only way for the experiment to work was for Robinson to stay above the fight. Robinson agreed.

The partnership of Robinson and Rickey is remarkable. They did a great thing together that neither could have done alone. Robinson would later say of Rickey that he was a "tough, shewed, courageous man."

(10) Robinson attended spring training with the Dodgers in 1946, but played with their minor league affiliate, Montreal, that year. Then in 1947 Jackie Robinson broke into the major leagues. He was confronted by racial slurs frequently that first year, but kept his promise to Rickey by not reacting. Other members of the Dodgers were won over to his defense, most notably "Pee Wee" Reese, the Dodgers star short stop and team captain from Kentucky.

(11) Robinson received death threats against himself and his family that first year with the Dodgers.

(12) Attendance at Dodger games both home and away increased in 1947, due to interest in Jackie Robinson.

(13) Robinson won the award for "National League Rookie of the Year" that first year and was selected to the National League All Star team.

(14) Robinson was selected for the National League All Star team a total of six years in his career.

(15) In 1949 Robinson won the batting championship of the National League and was named the Most Valuable Player in the league.

(16) Jackie Robinson's number 42 was officially retired from Major League Baseball to honor his play and his contribution to the game. He is the only player ever to have been so honored. There is now a famous Hollywood movie, *42*, about Robinson's struggle and accomplishments.

(17) Robinson was elected to the Baseball Hall of Fame in 1962.

(18) Jackie Robinson joined other African-American celebrities and more than 10,000 African-American students in Washington DC for the Youth March for Integration of Schools in 1958.

(19) Jackie Robinson died in 1972. He has since been posthumously awarded the Congressional Gold Medal and the Presidential Medal of Freedom.

Quotes from Jackie Robinson

A life is not important except in the impact it has on other lives.

I'm not concerned with your liking or disliking me... All I ask is that you respect me as a human being.

There's not an American in this country free until every one of us is free.

Life is not a spectator sport. If you're going to spend your whole life in the grandstand just watching what goes on, in my opinion you're wasting your life.

Earl Warren (1891-1974) and the Warren Court

(1) Earl Warren was Chief Justice of the US Supreme Court during a period when it issued some of the most revolutionary and important decisions it ever made. The best known of these are Brown vs. Board of Education, 1954, and Miranda vs. Arizona, 1966.

(2) Earl Warren served as a lieutenant in the army during World War I, but was never deployed oversees.

(3) A Republican politician, Warren served three terms as California governor and was the Republican candidate for Vice-President in 1948.

(4) Earl Warren was appointed as Chief Justice of the Supreme Court by President Eisenhower in 1953.

(5) As Chief Justice, Warren worked to achieve consensus decisions by his court.[73] The plethora[74] of consensus or near consensus decisions by the Warren Court enhanced the prestige of the court and the legitimacy of those decisions.

(6) In the most famous decision of the Warren Court, *Brown vs. Board of Education*, the court ruled that separate facilities could never be equal, because they imply by their nature that one group is superior to another.

(7) In the case of *Miranda* vs. *Arizona* the Warren court ruled that those arrested for a crime must be informed of their rights at the time of the arrest, and the state must provide a defense attorney for defendants unable for afford one themselves.

Quotes from Earl Warren

Many people consider the things government does for them to be social progress but they regard the things government does for others as socialism.

To get what you want, STOP doing what isn't working.

It is the spirit and not the form of law that keeps justice alive.

---

[73] Consensus: a unanimous decision.

[74] Plethora: great abundance, very many.

If it is a mistake of the head and not the heart don't worry about it, that's the way we learn.

Separate educational facilities are inherently unequal.

Thurgood Marshall (1908-1993), Separate is Not Equal

(1)   Thurgood Marshall was a long-time member of the NAACP and represented that organization in major federal cases, including some that went to the Supreme Court.

(2)   Marshall won fame as the lawyer who won the case of *Brown vs. Board of Education* in 1954. This is one of the most important decisions the Supreme Court ever made. Previous to this, the Supreme Court had ruled in 1896 (*Plessy vs. Ferguson*) that separate facilities for blacks and whites was legal, as long as they were equal. Marshall argued that separate facilities could never be equal because separation implied that one group was superior to another. He went on to argue that the psychological effects in small children were catastrophic.[75]

(3)   Thurgood Marshall was born in Baltimore, Maryland, the son of a railroad porter and the grandson of slaves.

(4)   Marshall excelled on his college debate team.

(5)   Marshall attended law school at Howard University. He graduated from Howard Law School first in his class.

(6)   Thurgood Marshall became the first African-American person appointed to the Supreme Court in 1967. He served with distinction on the Court from 1967 until 1991.

Quotes from Thurgood Marshall

In recognizing the humanity of our fellow beings, we pay ourselves the highest tribute.

---

[75] Catastrophic: disastrous.

None of us got where we are solely by pulling ourselves up by our bootstraps. We got here because somebody - a parent, a teacher, an Ivy League crony or a few nuns - bent down and helped us pick up our boots.

The measure of a country's greatness is its ability to maintain compassion in times of crisis.

You do what you think is right and let the law catch up.

Lawlessness is lawlessness. Anarchy is anarchy. Neither race nor color nor frustration is an excuse for lawlessness or anarchy.

Martin Luther King, Jr. (1929-1968) and the Victory of Reason

(1) Martin Luther King, Jr. was born in Atlanta, Georgia. He was the son of a Baptist Minister. Deep racial divisions plagued the United States during King's time. Racial segregation was enforced heavily in the states of the southeast and to a lesser extent in other states. Georgia and the other states of the former Confederacy were dangerous places for black people.

(2) MLK's father was strict and beat his son to discipline him until young Martin was 15 years old.

(3) Martin Luther King, Jr. earned a doctorate in Theology at Boston University.

(4) The 1950s and 1960s were a time when black frustration and anger were mounting. Most black leaders and many white leaders knew that fundamental change had to occur, but the methods to be used in achieving that change were debated. To some, violent resistance by white society seemed to call for violent action. MKL became the leader of those who advocated nonviolent resistance.

(5) King learned the tenets and techniques of nonviolent protest by studying the example of Mohandas Gandhi in India. Gandhi had used the ideas expressed by Henry David Thoreau in *On the Duty of Civil Disobedience.*

(6) MLK first gained fame for his involvement in the Montgomery (Alabama) Bus Boycott of 1955. A black woman, Rosa Parks, refused to give up her seat on a bus for a white man. Parks was arrested for violating the segregation law.

(7) Doctor King organized a boycott of the buses by black people. That boycott lasted more than a year. During that time, Doctor King's house was bombed. King, himself, was arrested. And the bus company nearly went bankrupt. The eventual results of the boycott were that the Supreme Court declared the bus segregation law unconstitutional and Martin Luther King, Jr. emerged as the dominate figure in the nonviolent protest movement.

(8) In 1957 Doctor King was among the founders of the Southern Christian Leadership Conference which he led until his death. Their goal was to focus moral authority on the active struggle for equal rights.

(9) MKL was nearly killed when he was stabbed in the chest by a mentally deranged black woman in Harlem. He was hospitalized and spent several weeks recovering.

(10) King led marches and sit-ins throughout the south and was frequently arrested and jailed. At times his children had to endure hearing their father called a "jail bird."

(11) At a King protest in Birmingham, Alabama, police turned fire hoses and dogs on the protesters when they refused to disburse. The incident was one of the first violent racial confrontations shown on television's nightly news. Many people were horrified by the actions of the police. This was an awakening moment in the equal rights movement. King was arrested. While in jail he wrote a now famous letter, "Letter from a Birmingham Jail," in which he detailed reasons why he was compelled to defy unreasonable laws.

(12) Doctor King led "the March on Washington" in 1963 at which he delivered his most famous speech, *I Have a Dream.*

(13) Doctor King was awarded the Nobel Peace Prize in 1964.

(14) After 1964 Doctor King began to address issues other than segregation. He came out against the Vietnam War and spoke about the need to address problems of poverty in the United States.

(15) Doctor King's birthday is celebrated as the holiday throughout the US on the third Monday of January. In some states it is called Civil Right Day.

(16) Doctor Martin Luther King was assassinated by a white racist in Memphis, Tennessee in 1968.

Quotes from Martin Luther King, Jr.

Life's most persistent and urgent question is, 'What are you doing for others?'

The function of education is to teach one to think intensively and to think critically. Intelligence plus character - that is the goal of true education.

Love is the only force capable of transforming an enemy into friend.

We must accept finite disappointment, but never lose infinite hope.

Darkness cannot drive out darkness; only light can do that. Hate cannot drive out hate; only love can do that.

In the end, we will remember not the words of our enemies, but the silence of our friends.

History will have to record that the greatest tragedy of this period of social transition was not the strident clamor of the bad people, but the appalling silence of the good people.

I have decided to stick with love. Hate is too great a burden to bear.

Injustice anywhere is a threat to justice everywhere.

I submit that an individual who breaks a law that conscience tells him is unjust, and who willingly accepts the penalty of imprisonment in order to arouse the conscience of the community over its injustice, is in reality expressing the highest respect for law.

Our lives begin to end the day we become silent about things that matter.

I look to a day when people will not be judged by the color of their skin, but by the content of their character.

The time is always right to do what is right.

Peace is not merely a distant goal that we seek, but a means by which we arrive at that goal.

Shirley Chisholm (1924-2005) Empowered

(1) Shirley Chisholm was born in Brooklyn, New York in 1924 to immigrant parents from the Caribbean region.

(2) Shirley Chisholm attended Brooklyn College where she participated on the debate team.

(3) Chisholm earned a master's degree in education in 1952 and worked as an educational consultant from 1952 to 1959.

(4) Chisholm was elected to the New York Assembly in 1964. Then in 1968 she became the first black woman elected to the US House of Representatives. She served 14 years (seven full terms) in the House from 1969 to 1983.

(5) In Congress, Chisholm worked on issues of nutrition and efforts to have federally supported child care, health care, and minimum wage.

(6) In 1971 Chisholm became a founding member of the Congressional Black Caucus and the National Women's Political Caucus.

(7) In 1972 Shirley Chisholm ran for the Democratic nomination for President and received 152 votes on the first ballot at the Democratic convention.

(8) After retiring from Congress, Chisholm taught political science and sociology at Mount Holy Oak (Women's) College and toured the United States speaking on issues of race and women's issues at colleges all over the country.

Quotes from Shirley Chisholm

At present, our country needs women's idealism and determination, perhaps more in politics than anywhere else.

Service is the rent that you pay for room on this earth.

Tremendous amounts of talent are lost to our society just because that talent wears a skirt.

In the end anti-black, anti-female, and all forms of discrimination are equivalent to the same thing: anti-humanism.

You don't make progress by standing on the sidelines, whimpering and complaining. You make progress by implementing ideas.

I am and always will be a catalyst for change.

Unless we start to fight and defeat the enemies in our own country, poverty and racism, and make our talk of equality and opportunity ring true, we are exposed in the eyes of the world as hypocrites when we talk about making people free.

Malcolm X (1925-1965) and Black Power

(1) Malcolm X, a prominent leader in the Nation of Islam, is one of the most important civil rights leaders of the twentieth century.

(2) Malcolm X was born Malcolm Little in Omaha, Nebraska in 1925.

(3) Malcolm Little's father, Earl, was somewhat of an activist in groups which encouraged black self-reliance and black pride. He was also an admirer of Marcus Garvey and Pan-Africanism.

(4) The family moved to Milwaukee, then to Lansing, Michigan.

(5) Malcolm's father was often in conflict with white racist groups. He was killed in an accident under some suspicious conditions when Malcolm was six years old. Malcolm's mother was

institutionalized for mental problems when Malcolm was 13. Malcolm came to live with his sister in Boston.

(6) Malcolm dropped out of school at around age 14 and had a variety of jobs thereafter.

(7) In 1943 Malcolm Little moved to Harlem and began a criminal career.

(8) In 1946 having returned to Boston and continued his life of petty crime, Little was caught, convicted, and sentenced to Charlestown State Prison where he served time until his release in 1953.

(9) While in prison Malcolm was encouraged by his bother Reginald to join the Nation of Islam. This was a religious-political movement led by Elijah Muhammad who preached that black people should separate themselves from white people and develop their own nation by investing in black owned businesses, avoiding doing business with whites, organizing black-Muslim schools, and encouraging black self-defense.

(10) There was an undeniably strong element of black racism in the movement. Elijah Muhammad taught that all white people were "devils" and advocated the use of violence.

(11) While in prison Malcolm began calling himself Malcolm X. The "X" referred to the unknown African identify which had been stolen from him and millions of others by abduction and slavery.

(12) When he was released from prison, Malcolm X visited Elijah Muhammad in Chicago and was commission by the leader to expand the movement in the large cities of the Eastern United States. Malcolm X then organized Temples in Detroit, Boston, Philadelphia, Harlem, and other cities. The movement gained strength under Malcolm, and he was becoming a more important figure in it than Elijah Muhammad.

(13) Under Malcolm X, community development and community self-help were emphasized, as well as a united protest against police brutality.

(14) Malcolm X explained the philosophy of his resistance movement like this: "Be peaceful, be courteous, obey the law, respect everyone; but if someone puts his hand on you, send him to the cemetery."

(15) In 1960 Malcolm X conferred with world leaders at United Nations, notably the leaders of several African nations and Fidel Castro of Cuba.

(16) Malcom X is credited with bringing the boxer, Cassius Clay, known today as Muhammad Ali, into the Nation of Islam and the two men were known to have been good friends.

(17) In later years, Malcolm X broke with the Nation of Islam because he believed that it had become corrupt and the leader, Elijah Muhammad, was not a good moral example.

(18) Malcolm X became Sunni Muslim after his break with Elijah Muhammad. Malcolm then went on the Hajj, the required pilgrimage to Mecca for all able Muslims, and through that experience he underwent a transformation. On returning to the United States he renounced all the racist teaching of the Nation of Islam in favor of the belief in equality of all people.

(19) After his Mecca trip, Malcom's leadership and organization was thought to be a threat to the Nation of Islam. He was assassinated by three Nation of Islam members in 1965. Elijah Muhammad denied that the three had acted on his orders.

(20) At the time of his death, Malcolm X was collaborating with author, Alex Haley, on *The Autobiography of Malcolm X*. Haley completed the work and published it shortly after Malcolm's death.

Quotes from Malcolm X

The media's the most powerful entity on earth. They have the power to make the innocent guilty and to make the guilty innocent, and that's power. Because they control the minds of the masses.

There is no better (experience) than adversity. Every defeat, every heartbreak, every loss, contains its own seed, its own lesson on how to improve your performance the next time.

Education is the passport to the future, for tomorrow belongs to those who prepare for it today.

I'm for truth, no matter who tells it. I'm for justice, no matter who it's for or against.

Nobody can give you freedom. Nobody can give you equality or justice or anything. If you're a man, you take it.

A man who stands for nothing will fall for anything.

You're not supposed to be so blind with patriotism that you can't face reality. Wrong is wrong, no matter who says it.

I believe in human beings, and that all human beings should be respected as such, regardless of their color.

To have once been a criminal is no disgrace. To remain a criminal is the disgrace.

History is a people's memory, and without a memory, man is demoted to the lower animals.

The true Islam has shown me that a blanket indictment of all white people is as wrong as when whites make blanket indictments against blacks.

Muhammad Ali (1942-2016), the Black Superman[76]

(1) Muhammad Ali was born Cassius Clay in Louisville, Kentucky in 1942. He changed his name to Muhammad Ali after converting to Islam as an adult.

(2) Cassius Clay won the Gold Medal for boxing in the light-heavyweight division of the 1960 Summer Olympic Games in Rome.

(3) In 1964 Cassius Clay defeat Sonny Liston to win the World Heavyweight boxing championship. The name change to Ali happened soon after this.

[76] Johnny Wakelin, "The Black Superman," Pye Records, 1974.

(4)   In 1967 Ali refused to be drafted into the US army. He was convicted of draft evasion, stripped of his title, and suspended from professional boxing.

(5)   In 1971 Ali's conviction was overturned by the Supreme Court, ruling that he was indeed a conscientious objector. He fought heavyweight champion Joe Frazier that year and lost the decision.

(6)   In 1974 Ali upset the favored Joe Frazier by a unanimous decision.

(7)   Ali was very vocal and verbally abusive of some opponents, notably Joe Frazier. He was also outspoken on the issues of race discrimination and the Vietnam War. In later years, as he matured, Ali seemed to be less inclined to boast or ridicule his opponents.

(8)   Ali won the Heavyweight Championship of the World for the second time by defeating the defending champion, George Foreman, in 1974. This was the "rumble in the jungle" fought in Zaire, and it was ten years after Ali had first won the championship.

(9)   Ali lost his title to Leon Spinks in a split decision in 1978. It was discovered later that Spinks had fractured Ali's jaw in the second round of the fight.

(10) Ali won a rematch with Spinks seven months after his loss, thus winning the heavyweight championship for the third time.

(11) Ali suffered from Parkinson's syndrome for many years. The disease is debilitating and causes the victim to shake uncontrollably. Ali and his family have denied that boxing was the cause, but Jerry Quarry, a boxing contemporary of Ali who fought Ali twice and fought all the same fighters Ali fought, had the same condition.

(12) Ali inspired many, especially young black men, to stand up and be proud of themselves.

Quotes from Muhammad Ali

Friendship... is not something you learn in school. But if you haven't learned the meaning of friendship, you really haven't learned anything.

I hated every minute of training, but I said, 'Don't quit. Suffer now and live the rest of your life as a champion.'

I know where I'm going and I know the truth, and I don't have to be what you want me to be. I'm free to be what I want. He who is not courageous enough to take risks will accomplish nothing in life.

I am an ordinary man who worked hard to develop the talent I was given. I believed in myself, and I believe in the goodness of others.

The word 'Islam' means 'peace.' The word 'Muslim' means 'one who surrenders to God.' But the press makes us seem like haters.

Only a man who knows what it is like to be defeated can reach down to the bottom of his soul and come up with the extra ounce of power it takes to win when the match is even.

The man who has no imagination has no wings.

Hating people because of their color is wrong. And it doesn't matter which color does the hating. It's just plain wrong.

A man who views the world the same at fifty as he did at twenty has wasted thirty years of his life.

I've made my share of mistakes along the way, but if I have changed even one life for the better, I haven't lived in vain.

Caesar Chavez (1927-1993), the Farm Workers, and More

(1) In 1962 Chavez cofounded the National Farm Workers Association. The name was later changed to the United Farm Workers.

(2) Caesar Chavez was born in 1927 in Yuma, Arizona. His family owned a grocery store and a ranch which they lost during the Great Depression.

(3) After losing their home in the economic downturn of 1929, the Chavez family moved to California and became migrant farm workers.

(4) Caesar Chavez dropped out of school in seventh grade to become a full-time farm worker and help his family survive.

(5) Chavez enlisted in the navy in 1944 at age 17 and served for two years.

(6) Chavez continued to work in the fields from 1946 until 1952. Then he became a community organizer supporting workers' rights and encouraging Latino-Americans to vote.

(7) In 1965 the United Farm Workers led a strike against California grape producers and encouraged a sympathetic boycott by all Americans. That strike would last for five years. In 1966 Senator Robert Kennedy, the brother of JFK, expressed support for the strike during Senate committee hearings. The grape strike inspired other strikes by farm workers and the growth of organized labor among farm workers.

(8) The California legislature passed the California Agricultural Labor Relations Act sanctioning the right of farm workers to organize in response to the UFW.

(9) Chavez famously fasted in support of various causes.[77] In 1968 he fasted for 25 days in support of "nonviolence"; in 1970 he fasted in "thanksgiving and hope" in support of farm workers; in 1972 he fasted in protest of an Arizona law forbidding farm workers from striking during harvest season.

(10) Caesar Chavez opposed illegal migration from Mexico because he said it undermined American workers while exploiting Mexicans.

(11) Caesar Chavez's birthday is a state holiday in California.

Quotes from Caesar Chavez

If you really want to make a friend, go to someone's house and eat with him... the people who give you their food give you their heart.

Preservation of one's own culture does not require contempt or disrespect for other cultures.

---

[77] Fast: to refrain from eating for an extended period of time.

We cannot seek achievement for ourselves and forget about progress and prosperity for our community... Our ambitions must be broad enough to include the aspirations and needs of others, for their sakes and for our own.

Students must have initiative; they should not be mere imitators. They must learn to think and act for themselves - and be free.

Real education should consist of drawing the goodness and the best out of our own students. What better books can there be than the book of humanity?

You are never strong enough that you don't need help.

Jaime Escalante (1930-2010) and a Disproof of Stereotyping in East LA

(1)   Jaime Escalante was born in Bolivia of indigenous American parents who were both teachers.

(2)   Escalante taught mathematics in Bolivia for several years before immigrating to the United States.

(3)   From 1974 until 1991 Escalante taught mathematics and science at a high school in economically depressed, mostly Latino, East Los Angeles.

(4)   The high school at which Escalante worked had been struggling with the threat of losing its accreditation due to poor student performance and a high dropout rate. While other teachers proposed lowering standards to meet the perceived needs of the students, Escalante proposed to offer Advanced Placement Calculus. ("AP" classes allow high school students to earn college credit by passing the AP test at the end of the course.)

(5)   Escalante spent his first few years raising the general level of achievement. In 1978 he taught the first AP Calculus class with five students. Two passed the AP test. The program kept expanding after that and gained national attention in 1982 when 18 of 18 AP calculus students passed the exam, but with answers and mistakes

markedly similar. Fourteen of the students were asked to take the exam again. Twelve agreed, and all twelve passed. The program expanded even more rapidly after the incident. In 1987, seventy-three students passed the AP Calculus exam.

(6) In 1988 Escalante was the subject of a book, *Escalante: The Best Teacher in America*, and a now famous movie, *Stand and Deliver.* The movie exaggerated the accomplishment, but Escalante's accomplish and those of his students were nothing less than incredible.

(7) By Escalante's last year at Garfield High School in East Los Angeles the school could boast more than 500 students taking AP classes in a single year.

Quotes by Jaime Escalante

There will be no free rides, no excuses. You already have two strikes against you: your name and your complexion. Because of those two strikes, there are some people in this world who will assume that you know less than you do. *Math* is the great equalizer... When you go for a job, the person giving you that job will not want to hear your problems; ergo, neither do I. You're going to work harder here than you've ever worked anywhere else. And the only thing I ask from you is *ganas.* *Desire.*

Tough guys don't do math. Tough guys fry chicken for a living.

Gloria Steinem (1934-present) and Equality for Women

(1) Gloria Steinem's parents divorced when she was 10 years old. She continued to live with her mother who was mentally unstable and would be institutionalized for an extended period twice.

(2) After college Steinem spent two years in India on a fellowship study.

(3) In 1960 Steinem began her career in journalism.

(4) In 1962 Steinem wrote an article for *Esquire* which came to be used as the introduction to Betty Friedan's book, *The Feminine Mystique.*

(5) In 1963 Steinem was employed as a Bunny at the Playboy Mansion. She wrote an article called "A Bunny's Tale", which was published

in *Show* magazine in which she detailed what she considered the exploitation of the women who worked at the mansion.

(6)   Steinem focused on women's issues in much of her writing.

(7)   In 1971 Steinem was among the cofounders of the National Women's Political Caucus. And she supported Shirley Chisholm's Presidential bid in 1972.

(8)   In 1972 Steinem cofounded *Ms. Magazine.*

(9)   In 1984 Steinem, other activists, and some Congressmen were arrested for disorderly conduct during a protest against apartheid outside the South African embassy in Washington, DC.[78]

(10) Steinem publicly opposed the Gulf War in 1991.

(11) In the early 1990s Steinem coproduced and narrated documentary films on women's issues for television.

Quotes from Gloria Steinem

A gender-equal society would be one where the word 'gender' does not exist: where everyone can be themselves.

Without leaps of imagination, or dreaming, we lose the excitement of possibilities. Dreaming, after all, is a form of planning.

Power can be taken, but not given. The process of the taking is empowerment in itself.

The most hurtful thing is not what comes from our adversaries, it's what comes from our friends.

If you say, I'm for equal pay, that's a reform. But if you say. I'm a feminist, that's a transformation of society.

Most American children suffer too much mother and too little father.

A pedestal is as much a prison as any small, confined space.

---

[78] Apartheid: the forced separation of races with a privileged race in political power. Apartheid was the basis of the organization of South African society at that time.

I'm so happy that we're finally hearing the stories and voices of women who make America. We do what we see, not what we're told, so an incomplete story of this country damages everyone.

Law and justice are not always the same.

Wilma Mankiller (1945-2010), Cherokee Pride and Feminism

(1) Wilma Mankiller, the first female Principal Chief of the Cherokee Nation, was a progressive leader who preached and inspired self-determination.

(2) Wilma Mankiller was born on the Cherokee Reservation in Oklahoma in 1945. She had ten siblings and no electricity or indoor plumbing.

(3) Wilma's family moved to San Francisco under a Bureau of Indian Affairs relocation program in 1956.

(4) Mankiller married an Ecuadorian immigrant in 1963 and had two daughters from that marriage.

(5) Wilma Mankiller participated in the indigenous occupation of Alcatraz Island, which became a rallying point for the modern American Indian Rights Movement.

(6) Mankiller's activism in the Indian Rights Movement displeased her husband. This led the couple to divorce in 1977, whereupon, Mankiller took her two daughters and returned to her Oklahoma Reservation.

(7) Upon her return to the reservation, Wilma Mankiller and her daughters found themselves homeless. In the beginning they lived in a tent while Wilma looked for work.

(8) Wilma Mankiller became active in government on the Cherokee Reservation, but a severe automobile accident in 1979 took Mankiller out of government service for nearly two years during which she was recovering.

(9) After returning to Cherokee government service, Wilma Mankiller so impressed Principal Chief Ross Swimmer that he

chose her as his running mate in the position of Assistant Chief. The nomination of a woman as Assistant Chief created anger, resentment, and threats of violence. Swimmer and Mankiller won the election with 50.4% of the vote.

(10) When Ross Swimmer went off to Washington as Assistant Secretary in the Bureau of Indian Affairs, Wilma Mankiller became the first female Principal Chief. She met substantial opposition in her first bid for reelection simply because she was a woman. But when she ran again in 1985, she received 80% of the vote.

(11) Of the 500 plus indigenous nations within the United States, the Cherokee is the second largest.

(12) Mankiller initiated projects on the Cherokee Reservation and encouraged tribal members to participate in their own development, as well as tribal decision making.

(13) Wilma Mankiller supported bringing gaming to the Cherokee Reservation as a source of revenue to be used to build thing like health care facilities for the Cherokee. She also encouraged Cherokee tribal members to fill positions in tribal health care facilities as physicians, nurses, dentists, etc., and found ways to support candidates with scholarships. When she left office, the Cherokee Nation was moving toward modernization with a renewed sense of pride and a healthy respect for women.

(14) Wilma Mankiller was selected as *Ms. Magazine's* Woman of the Year in 1987.

(15) Wilma Mankiller was awarded the Presidential Medal of Freedom in 1998. She has also been honored by selection in the Oklahoma Women's Hall of Fame.

(16) Wilma Mankiller's autobiography, *Mankiller: A Chief and Her People*, was a national bestseller.

(17) Wilma Mankiller retired from politics due to multiple serious physical ailments. She survived a kidney transplant only to be diagnosed with pancreatic cancer from which she eventually died.

Quotes from Wilma Mankiller

In Iroquois society, leaders are encouraged to remember seven generations in the past and consider seven generations in the future when making decisions that affect the people.

I don't think anybody anywhere can talk about the future of their people or of an organization without talking about education. Whoever controls the education of our children controls our future.

We must trust our own thinking. Trust where we're going. And get the job done.

America would be a better place if leaders would do more long-term thinking.

Prior to my election, young Cherokee girls would never have thought that they might grow up and become chief.

I want to be remembered as the person who helped us restore faith in ourselves.

I've run into more discrimination as a woman than as an Indian.

CHAPTER 16

COLD WAR—PART II, 1964-1994

The Vietnam War

The Cold War mindset, around which American foreign policy was decided, had some disastrous results. The most notable of these was the Vietnamese War. After World War II, the communist Ho Chi Minh led an armed rebellion against French colonial rule in Vietnam. When the French were defeat in 1954, rival communist and anticommunist supporters agreed to a temporary partition of Vietnam at the 17th parallel. The north would be communist under Ho Chi Minh; the south would be noncommunist under Ngo Dinh Diem. Elections were to be held in 1956 to reunite the country.

But Diem, certain that he would lose, refused to hold the election in 1956, declaring South Vietnam an independent country and calling on the United States for help. American leaders feared that if Vietnam became communist this would lead to neighboring countries becoming communist.[79] Though the South Vietnamese government under Diem was corrupt and evil, it received US financial support, military equipment, and military advisors. The logic was that as long as that government was not communist, there would be hope of reform one day; but if the communists took over, the country would be lost forever.

---

[79] This is the "domino theory" which pervaded American Cold War policy; that countries would fall like a line of dominos once one country in a region became communist. The American reaction was to support any noncommunist resistance, no matter how corrupt or how evil.

US involvement in Vietnam had begun under President Eisenhower and continued under President Kennedy. At the time of Kennedy's death, there were 15 thousand US military personnel in Vietnam. They were supposed to have been strictly limited to advising only, but they were actively engaged in combat, and their role was increasing. Ironically, shortly before Kennedy's assassination, Diem was assassinated by some of his top generals. This should have caused the US to investigate and rethink American involvement in Vietnam, but President Johnson, Kennedy's successor, could not see past the "domino theory."

While South Vietnam floundered with a series of military dictators over the next several years, President Johnson extended the American commitment to that country. A major turning point came in August 1964 when an American naval vessel was engaged by North Vietnamese vessels in the Gulf of Tonkin, off the coast of North Vietnam. President Johnson claimed that the American vessel had been attacked in international waters, and he asked Congress to give him the authority to direct military operations without a US declaration of war and without the consent of Congress. Johnson claimed that he needed this flexibility in order to be able to deal with situations like that which had just occurred. Congress agreed and passed the Gulf of Tonkin Resolution. Johnson then used this authority to direct American forces to engage in direct combat operations in Vietnam. Unchecked by Congress, Johnson greatly increased the number of US troops in Vietnam. By 1968 there were more than 500,000 American troops in that small country. The war was now between the Vietcong rebels and North Vietnamese on one side and the US and its South Vietnamese ally on the other. The military of South Vietnam, however, was becoming increasingly irrelevant.

Richard Nixon was elected President in 1968, pledging that he had a plan to extricate the US from Vietnam. That plan turned out to be "Vietnamization". Nixon hoped to train an effective South Vietnamese army to take over the war against the communists while gradually reducing American troop strength in Vietnam. Nixon did in fact reduce the number of American troops in Vietnam significantly but very gradually. When Nixon ran for reelection in 1972, American troops were still fighting in Vietnam and 20,000 more Americans had died in Vietnam during Nixon's first term. Vietnam had become America's longest war up to that time, and American involvement would not end completely until 1975.

Frustration with the Vietnam War became the main cause of the development of a youth counterculture in America during the 1960s and early 1970s: one that rejected capitalist values, indulged in narcissism, and flaunted the law.[80]

The Counterculture in Song

Because music was an intricate part of the counterculture, the story of the counterculture is best told in song.

Bob Dylan, 1941-present

Bob Dylan was born Robert Zimmerman in 1941 in Duluth, Minnesota. He changed his name to Dylan to honor the poet Dylan Thomas who influenced him. In 1961 he migrated to New York City where he gained fame as a singer-songwriter of contemporary folk music. His two biggest early hits, *Blowin' in the Wind* and *The Times They Are a Changin'* set a tone and a standard for other protest singers soon to come.

Blowin' in the Wind

How many roads must a man walk down
Before they call him a man?
How many seas must a white dove sail
Before she sleeps in the sand?
How many times must the cannon balls fly
Before they're forever banned?
The answer, my friend, is blowing in the wind
The answer is blowing in the wind....

---

[80] Narcissism: excessive interest in one's own appearance and comfort (from the ancient Greek fable of Narcissus).

The Times They Are a Changin'

Come gather 'round people
Wherever you roam
And admit that the waters
Around you have grown...

... Then you better start swimmin'
Or you'll sink like a stone
For the times they are a-changin,

In another, less well known of his works, *God on Our Side*, Dylan comments on America's Indian Wars, the Spanish-American War, and both World Wars before honing in on his own time with the following lines:

God on Our Side

... But now we got weapons
Of the chemical dust
If fire them we're forced to
Then fire them we must
One push of the button
And a shot the world wide
And you never ask questions
When God's on your side....

Phil Ochs and Tom Paxton, Greenwich Village Stars

Bob Dylan was the Greenwich Village folksinger who became universally famous, but he was not the only talented young writer in Greenwich Village with something to say. At least two of his contemporaries wrote compelling folk songs with themes that challenged the establishment ideology.

Phil Ochs gained moderate fame with his antiwar songs *Too Many Martyrs*; *I Ain't Marching Anymore*; and *Draft Dodger Rag*. Ochs was a fan of Woody Guthrie and Guthrie's influence is clear in *Power and the Glory*, a beautiful, upbeat, and patriotic song by Ochs. Ochs was impatient and depressed when his career did not take off. Sadly, he took his own life in 1976.

The other Greenwich Village star on the rise in the early 1960s was Tom Paxton who would write more than one song about Vietnam. His *What did you Learn in School Today?* mocks the simple, patriot lies that children are often taught. *Get Up Jimmy Newman* had a much darker tone. Paxton has written a wide variety of music. A notable subset of his works are social/political commentary. *The White Bones of Allende,* which suggests American involvement with an assassination in Chile, is a classic example of this side of Paxton. The lyrics implore Americans to know and care about what their government is doing. Paxton still performs today, and he has a loyal following. Many of the songs he has written have been performed by well-known celebrities.

Crosby, Stills, and Nash, the American Super Group of the 60s

When David Crosby joined with Stephen Stills and Graham Nash to form CSN all three had already made their marks in the popular music world. Crosby had been the lead singer of the Byrds, a popular country-folk-pop band. Stephen Stills had been a member of Buffalo Springfield, the group famous for its iconic counterculture hit "For What It's Worth". And Graham Nash had been the lead singer of The Hollies, a top pop British band. This super-group was later joined by Neil Young, who had been with Stephen Still as a fellow member of Buffalo Springfield, and was, himself, a popular solo star.

Two songs by CSN&Y and one by Graham Nash, solo, chronicle significant events in American history. The Graham Nash song, *Chicago, We Can Change the World,* is a sympathetic portrayal of the plight of Black Panther Bobby Seale who was charged with inciting a riot during the Vietnam War protests at the Democratic National Convention in Chicago in 1968. Seale was so loud in his protests during his trial that he was ordered bound and gagged.

Ohio by CSN&Y is a response to the news in 1970 that four students protesting the Vietnam War at Kent State University in Ohio were shot and killed by National Guard troops called in to keep order.

Woodstock, which was actually written by Joni Mitchell but recorded by CSN&Y, celebrates the minor miracle of the Woodstock Music Festival of 1969. The promoters of the three day outdoor event severely underestimated the potential crowd and potential problems. They had planned for no more than 200,000 people, but nearly 500,000 showed up. Conditions at the event would be stressful, possibly miserable. The chances for disaster and likelihood of multiple lawsuits drove the promoters to stress to the audience that the world would be watching, and this was a chance to prove that people could be better than what was commonly believed. The appeal for civility was successful. Rain that weekend made the Woodstock Festival a muddy mess, but spirits were high, and there were few incidences of any problems. Mitchell was not actually at the event, but CSN were there performing.

Here are excerpts from the iconic songs mentioned above:

For What It's Worth by Buffalo Springfield

Somethin' happenin' here
What it is ain't exactly clear
There's a man with a gun over there
Tellin' me I got to beware....

... What a field day for the heat![81]
Thousand people in the street
Singin' songs and carryin' signs
Mostly say "Hurray for our side."

Chicago, We Can Change the World by Graham Nash

So your brother's bound and gagged
And they've chained him to a chair.
Won't you please come to Chicago
Just to sing?
In a land that's known as "freedom"

---

[81] "The heat" was slang for the police.

How can such a thing be fair?
Won't you please come to Chicago
For the help that you can bring?

Ohio by Crosby, Stills, Nash, and Young

Tin soldiers and Nixon's comin'
We're finally on our own.
This summer I hear the drummin'
Four dead in Ohio.

Gotta get down to it.
Soldiers are cutting us down.
Should have been done long ago.

Woodstock written by Joni Mitchell and performed by CSN&Y

By the time we got to Woodstock
We were half a million strong
And everywhere was a song
And a celebration.

We are stars
And we know just who we are.
And we got to get ourselves
Back to the garden....

"Country Joe" McDonald and the Anthem of the Counter-culture

Country Joe McDonald, who is known for little else, had perhaps the most iconic performance at Woodstock with a song that became something of an anthem for the Vietnam War protest movement from that time forward with the *I-Feel-Like-I'm-Fixin'-To-Die Rag*.

I-Feel-Like-I'm-Fixin'-To-Die Rag by Country Joe and the Fish

Well come on all you big, strong men
Uncle Sam needs your help again.
Got himself in a terrible jam
Way down yonder in Vietnam

So put down your books
And pick up a gun.
We're gonna have
A whole lot of fun.

John Prine

Near the end of the war, some new folk singers were picking up the antiwar theme. John Prine is one who stands out. He often wrote with insight and sarcasm. His song *Sam Stone* (1971) is about PTSD before the term was in common us.[82]

Sam Stone by John Prine

Sam Stone
Came home
To his wife and family
After serving in the conflict oversees...

... But the morphine eased the pain
And the grass grew round his brain
And gave him all the confidence he lacked
With a Purple Heart and a monkey on his back.[83]

---

[82] PTSD is post-traumatic stress syndrome, a mental health problem caused by experiencing a terrifying event. This is a common problem in war veterans. The condition had been recognized since World War I when it was known as "shell shock."

[83] Purple Heart: the military award presented to those wounded in combat.

1968: Turmoil[84]

Turmoil, no other word better described the events of 1968 in the United States. President Lyndon Johnson had become so unpopular because of the Vietnam War that he soon was forced to realize that he had no chance of being re-elected. So he announced that he would not seek another term. Vice-president Hubert Humphrey was the establishment Democratic favorite and he was a good man. But his connection with the Johnson administration and the increasingly more unpopular Vietnam War made him vulnerable to a challenge. The little known Minnesota Senator, Eugene McCarthy, (not related to the infamous Senator Joseph McCarthy) decided to run for President as an antiwar candidate and did well in early Democratic primary elections. With the Democratic nomination seemingly up for grabs, New York Senator and former US Attorney General Robert Kennedy, brother of the late President Kennedy, decided to run, bringing vitality and an agenda of social reforms into the race.

Martin Luther King had been assassinated in April. There were riots in major cities. Then Robert Kennedy was assassinated in July, the evening after he had won the California primary and seemed to be on his way to the Democratic nomination. By the time the Democratic Convention met in Chicago later that summer, Humphrey had won enough delegates in the primary elections to be nearly certain of the nomination.

Because of the war and Humphrey's connection to President Johnson, thousands of protestors descended upon Chicago for the Convention. The Chicago police met the protesters with such angry physical force that a subsequent federal government investigation of the events of those days called the confrontations a "police riot." Hundreds of protesters were beaten and many arrests were made. One of those arrested was Bobby Seale of whose trial Graham Nash later wrote *Chicago, We Can Change the World.* Hubert Humphrey did get the Democratic nomination that year, but was defeated by Richard Nixon who pledged to restore the rule of law and get the US out of Vietnam.

---

[84] Turmoil: Chaos, disorder, confusion.

Robert F. Kennedy (1925-1968), Hope and Tragedy

(1) Robert F. Kennedy was the younger brother of President John F. Kennedy and the older brother of long-time Massachusetts Senator Edward "Ted" Kennedy.

(2) Robert Kennedy is commonly known by his initials RFK.

(3) Robert Kennedy graduated from Harvard University and the University of Virginia Law School.

(4) Robert Kennedy served in the Navy briefly 1945-46.

(5) Robert Kennedy's first government service was as special counsel to the Senate Labor Rackets Committee investigating organized crime 1957-59.

(6) In 1960 Robert Kennedy was the campaign manager for his brother, John's successful Presidential campaign.

(7) John F. Kennedy appointed his brother, Robert F. Kennedy as US Attorney General. Robert continued in that position under President Lyndon Johnson for a year, but resigned because of strong disagreement over the Vietnam War and to run for Senate.

(8) As Attorney General, Kennedy consistently supported the rights of civil rights protestors and African-Americans challenging racial discrimination in the South.

(9) Robert Kennedy served as US Senator from New York from 1965 until his death in 1968.

(10) Robert Kennedy was a leading candidate for the Democratic nomination for President in 1968.

(11) Robert Kennedy was assassinated after winning the California Democratic Presidential Primary Election. He was running on a platform of ending the Vietnam War and expanding efforts to eliminate poverty in the United States. Some people speculate that his election as President would have turned America in an entirely different and better direction than it went.

Quotes from Robert F. Kennedy

There are those who look at things the way they are, and ask why... I dream of things that never were, and ask why not?

Only those who dare to fail greatly can ever achieve greatly.

Few will have the greatness to bend history itself; but each of us can work to change a small portion of events, and in the total; of all those acts will be written the history of this generation.

The Last Years of the Cold War

President Nixon, though much maligned, was a skilled politician and can be credited with helping to end the Cold War.[85] Détente was established with the Soviet Union.[86] And Nixon actually went to China and began normalized relation between China and the US for the first time. Nixon's Vietnamization program worked to the extent that American troop strength in Vietnam was greatly reduced in time for the 1972 Presidential election.

On the other hand, it was becoming increasingly more obvious that the Vietnam War would be lost. Americans and Vietnamese were losing their lives or having their lives destroyed for no apparent reason. Nixon also expanded the war by allowing American airstrikes into neighboring Cambodia. Cambodia had been used as a safe-haven by Vietcong (communist insurgents) for raids across the border into Vietnam. The airstrikes were planned to deal with the problem. But what they ended up doing was to draw Cambodia into the war. The result for Cambodia was unimaginable disaster and misery. The stress of the financial cost of the war was also negatively affecting the US economy. Crime may have been reduced, but respect for the law was low, especially among the young of the counterculture.

The Democratic Presidential nomination was hotly contested in 1972 and not fully decided until the convention itself. As a result, the Democratic nominee, George McGovern, emerged without strong party support. McGovern's campaign also received a severe setback when McGovern's choice for Vice-president was found to have had psychological counselling for person problems and had to be removed from the ticket. But the

[85] Maligned: highly criticized.

[86] Détente: an understanding of cooperation and truce.

McGovern campaign had a much greater vulnerability, McGovern made withdrawal from the Vietnam War the centerpiece of his entire platform with little mention of any unrelated issues. About two weeks before the election, President Nixon's Secretary of State, Henry Kissinger, announced that the end of American involvement in Vietnam was imminent.[87]

Nixon crushed McGovern in the election, winning 49 of the 50 states, but he did not enjoy his victory for long. In the course of the campaign a member of Nixon's reelection committee, had authorized a break-in of Democratic Headquarters in the Watergate Building in Washington, D.C. The burglars were caught and President Nixon was informed of the incident. Nixon tried to engineer a cover-up and wait for the issues to be forgotten. But it was not forgotten, and President Nixon continued the cover-up involving many members of his staff. The investigation lasted well over a year and eventually led to impeachment proceedings against the President.[88]

In the meantime, Nixon's Vice-president had also been charged with an unrelated crime, forced to resign, and later convicted. This complicated the situation because the office of Vice-president was vacant, and the Vice-president is the official who takes over the presidency should that office become vacant. Nixon was allowed to select the next Vice-president knowing that his selection would likely become President. The impeachment process went to a vote in the House of Representatives. The House voted to move the process forward to the next step, which would have been a trial in the Senate. At that point President Nixon resigned.

Vice-president Gerald Ford was elevated to the Presidency. Ford is still today unique among American Presidents as the only one who was never elected to either the Presidency or the Vice-presidency. Ford's first official act on assuming the Presidency was to grant a full pardon to Richard Nixon for any crimes which he may have committed while President. The oddest thing about this is that pardons are issued to criminals after they have been convicted. President Ford asserted that his action in issuing the pardon was to help put the issue of Richard Nixon in the past so

---

[87] Imminent: about to happen very soon.

[88] Impeachment: the formal procedure for removing an official from office for a serious crime. The procedure involves a trial in the Senate.

that the country could move on. This was probably true. Ford was well respected for his integrity, but the appearance of corruption may have hurt his bid for reelection in 1976. James "Jimmy" Carter defeat Ford for the Presidency that year, promising never to lie to the American people.

James Earl "Jimmy" Carter (1924-present), America's Most Successful Ex-President

(1) Jimmy Carter was born in rural Georgia. His father was a peanut farmer who owned a general store.

(2) Jimmy Carter graduated from the US Naval Academy in Annapolis, Maryland in 1946. And served as a naval officer until 1953.

(3) Carter served in the nuclear submarine division of the Navy from 1952 to 1953 and was involved in the clean-up of a nuclear accident in Canada. This experience caused him to always be wary of the use of nuclear energy.

(4) After resigning from the Navy to attend to the family business, Jimmy Carter was relatively poor and lived in government subsidized housing for three years.

(5) Carter served two terms as a Georgia State Senator and one term as Georgia Governor before running for President.

(6) Carter was an unpopular President because of his inabilities to cope with an economic crisis and the Iranian Hostage Crisis. The problems of the American economy had been growing for years. President Nixon had resorted to temporary wage and price controls without dealing directly with the situation. Government deficit spending was causing hyperinflation and this in turn was causing stagnation.[89]

The Iranian Hostage Crisis resulted when a revolution occurred in Iran while the Shaw (dictator) of Iran was in the United States for cancer treatment. The revolutionaries overran the American

---

[89] Inflation: a condition rapidly increasing prices and wages.
Stagnation: in economic terms, a condition of lack of economic growth often characterized by high levels of unemployment in the economy.

Embassy in Tehran and took 50 Americans hostage. They demanded the return of the Shaw in exchange for the hostages. The Shaw was an American ally who would have been prosecuted and probably executed if returned, so the US could not agree to turn him over.

(7) President Carter did have a major foreign policy achievement by getting the leaders of Israel and Egypt—mortal enemies—to sign a peace agreement, the Camp David Accords. This also opened the way for future negotiation and agreements between Israel and its Arab neighbors.

(8) Carter was defeated in his reelection bid in 1980 by Republican Ronald Reagan.

(9) After returning to Georgia, former President Jimmy Carter opened the Carter Center in Atlanta, Georgia for the purpose of promoting world peace, human rights, and world understanding. The Carter Center remains very active in efforts to settle international disputes and monitor elections.

(10) Former President Carter has actively participated in Habitat for Humanity projects helping to build affordable houses all over the world. And he has done much to promote awareness and support of the program.

(11) Jimmy Carter was awarded the Nobel Peace Prize in 2002 for his many efforts and successes all over the world.

(12) Carter has worked tirelessly in his effort to help find a solution to the Arab-Israeli Conflict and has written several books on the subject.

(13) Jimmy Carter has written more than 20 books on a variety of subjects.

(14) At the time of this writing former President Jimmy Carter had just been diagnosed with cancer at the age of 90.

Quotes from Jimmy Carter

You can do what you have to do, and sometimes you can do it even better than you think you can.

Human rights is the soul of our foreign policy, because human rights is the very soul of our sense of nationhood.

America did not invent human rights. In a very real sense human rights invented America.

We have a tendency to condemn people who are different from us, to define their sins as paramount and our own sinfulness as being insignificant.

I hate to see complacency prevail in our lives when it's so directly contrary to the teaching of Christ.

If you fear making anyone mad, then you ultimately probe for the lowest common denominator of human achievement.

President Ronald Reagan (1911-2004) and Morning in America

(1) Ronald Reagan was born to a relatively poor family in northern Illinois in 1911. His father was a salesman.

(2) Reagan worked as a lifeguard at a beach for six summers and prided himself in the fact that he had saved many people from drowning. He often sited this accomplishment as being what he was most proud of.

(3) Reagan attended Eureka College in Illinois where he was a cheer leader, a football player, captain of the swim team, and student body president.

(4) After college Reagan first became a sports announcer in Iowa.

(5) Ronald Reagan moved to Hollywood in 1937 and became an actor. He was featured in many "B" movies, and starred in several.

(6) Ronald Reagan costarred with a chimpanzee in "Bedtime for Bonzo" in 1951.

(7) Ronald Reagan had been a member of the Army Reserves since 1937 and was called to active duty in 1942. Poor eyesight limited him to state-side duty throughout the war, so he was assigned to make films for the army.

(8)   Ronald Reagan was President of the Screen Actors Guild from 1947 to 1952 and again in 1959.

(9)   Ronald Reagan had been a Democrat until 1962. At that time he switched to the Republican Party.

(10) In 1964 Ronald Reagan endorsed Barry Goldwater for President of the United States, and appeared in a campaign advertisement for Goldwater. Reagan's powerful screen presence in that ad caused California Republican Party leaders to consider Reagan as a future candidate for some high office.

(11) Ronald Reagan was elected Governor of California in 1966 and served as Governor until 1975.

(12) In 1976 Ronald Reagan challenged incumbent President Gerald Ford for the Republican presidential nomination and almost won.

(13) In 1980 Ronald Reagan was elected President of the United States, defeating incumbent President Jimmy Carter.

(14) President Reagan was the only divorcee to ever become President until the election of Donald Trump.

(15) The fifty American hostages in Iran were released on Ronald Reagan's inauguration day. They had been held for 444 days.

(16) President Reagan was shot in the chest in an assassination attempt by a mentally ill young man in 1981. The bullet lodged near his heart, but it was removed and within weeks he made a full recovery. He lived to be America's oldest President and broke the infamous "20 year curse" that had haunted the Presidency since 1840.[90]

(17) Faced with a desperately struggling economy, President Reagan made the tough choice to allow a deep recession to occur without government interference. The recession lasted a year and President Reagan's popularity plummeted, but the economy bounced back in a healthier condition than it had been in years.

(18) President Reagan emphasized deregulation of industry and reduction of government involvement in the economy saying that

---

[90] "The 20 year curse": Beginning in 1840, every President elected on the even 20 years of the century had died in office. 1840—Zachary Taylor-poisoned maybe deliberately; 1860—Lincoln assassinated; 1880—James Garfield assassinated; 1900—William McKinley assassinated; 1920—Warren G. Harding heart attack; 1940—FDR stroke; 1960 JFK assassinated.

"Government is not the solution; government is the problem." The President also wanted to reduce government spending and did in many areas, but he increased military spending much more, contributing to an increase in the national debt.

(19) President Reagan's foreign policy was often predicated on the old Cold War assumption that any government was better than a communist government. This led to interference with the elected communist government of Nicaragua and American support for an undemocratic, corrupt government in El Salvador. Both of these adventures proved embarrassing for the United States.

(20) President Reagan negotiated an arms reduction agreement with the Soviet Union.

(21) President Reagan's last six years in office were years of robust economic growth in America.

(22) First Lady Nancy Reagan was influential in her husband's administration. She was also a firm believer in astrology, and advised her husband accordingly.

(23) A major scandal late in President Reagan's second term tarnished his Presidency. Illegal activities, poor judgement, and lack of proper oversight were all part of the Iran-Contra Scandal, and there was enough evidence to suggest that crimes had been committed. But the incident grew from overzealousness, rather than self-interest. The public and the Republican Congress turned out to be willing to look the other way and allow a popular President to gracefully exit the White House.

(24) Former President Reagan was diagnosed with Alzheimer's disease in 1994. For the next ten years he was kept out of the public eye and cared for by his wife, Nancy.

Quotes from Ronald Reagan

We can't help everyone, but everyone can help someone.

When you can't make them see the light, make them feel the heat.

Heroes may not be braver than anyone else. They're just braver five minutes longer.

CHAPTER 17

THE EXTENSION OF AMERICAN HEGEMONY IN THE TWENTY-FIRST CENTURY

Hegemony is a position of leadership or dominance by one country or society. It is not achieved by having the strongest military or the most wealth. The world follows because they want to. Hegemony is achieved through innovation, creativity, and ideas which matter. American hegemony thus far in the twenty-first century has resulted from innovations in computer technology and use, dominance in the entertainment industry, and philanthropy on a scale never before seen.[91] The world follows because the bright light of America is showing a better way.

Bill Gates (1955-present), Changing the World

(1) Bill Gates was born in Seattle Washington to an upper middle class family. His father was a lawyer and his mother was on the board of directors of the First Interstate BancSystem and the United Way.

(2) Bill went to a private school where he had access to computers at a time when most students did not. He was even excused from math class to work on computer programming.

(3) Gates did not have unlimited access to computer time, as we do today. In fact one summer he and three other high school

---

[91] Philanthropy: a desire to help mankind, especially through gifts and generosity.

boys were banned from access to computers at a local center for hacking the system in order to get unauthorized extra computer time. After the ban, the four boys went to work at that center to find bugs and improve the system.

(4) Gates began his career as a computer programmer while in high school and had written several commercial programs before high school graduation.

(5) Gates graduated from high school in 1973 as a National Merit Scholar.

(6) Gates scored 1590 out of a possible 1600 on his SAT test.

(7) Bill Gates served as a page in the US House of Representatives in 1973.

(8) Bill Gates attended Harvard for two years, during which he continued to concentrate on computer programming.

(9) Gates dropped out of Harvard to establish Microsoft.

(10) Microsoft was accused of monopolistic practices, found to be in violation of the Sherman Anti-trust Act, and forced to make policy changes which allowed its competitors access to markets which Gates had effectively blocked.

(11) Microsoft systems continued to offer a high quality operating system and continued to improve the system with Gates in charge, thus continuing to dominate the market by outcompeting others.

(12) On New Year's Day 1994 Bill Gates married Melinda French. Melinda had been the valedictorian of her high school class. She has a master's degree from Duke University. She was employed as a product developer with Microsoft at the time the couple met. The couple have three children and Melinda is a fully engaged partner in the couple's philanthropic endeavors.

(13) Bill Gates' wealth continued to grow. He would become the richest man in the world.

(14) In 2000 Bill Gates and Melinda founded the Bill and Melinda Gates Foundation to oversee donations to philanthropic agencies and projects. This foundation is the wealthiest philanthropic institution ever in all human history. The Gates have stated that their goal is to give away 95% of their wealth to causes which will benefit humanity. The Foundation has already had a major

impact on health projects in Africa. The Gates have focused the Foundation on four world development needs. These are: health, education (especially for girls), agricultural improvement, and institutional lending to small entrepreneurs.

Quotes from Bill Gates

It's fine to celebrate success but it is more important to heed the lessons of failure.

I think it's fair to say that personal computers have become the most empowering tool we've ever created. They're tools of communication, they're tools of creativity, and they can be shaped by their user.

We always overestimate the change that will occur in the next two years and underestimate the change that will occur in the next ten.

As we look ahead into the next century, leaders will be those who empower others.

By improving health, empowering women, population growth comes down.

I believe the returns on investment in the poor are just as exciting as successes achieved in the business arena, and they are even more meaningful!

Exposure from a young age to the realities of the world is a super-big thing.

Steve Jobs (1955-2011), Inventing and Re-inventing the Apple

(1)   Steve Jobs did not know his biological parents well. He was adopted at birth in San Francisco, California.
(2)   Steve's biological father was a graduate student from Syria while his biological mother was a professor at the University of Wisconsin.

(3) Neither of Steve's adopted parents had attended college (university). Steve's adopted father had not even graduated from high school and worked as a "repo man".[92]

(4) The Los Altos, California home, where Steve Jobs lived as a teenager and young man and later founded Apple Computers, has been declared a National Historic Site.

(5) Steve Jobs was employed as an assembler for Hewitt-Packard during the summer when he was 13 years old.

(6) Steve Jobs did not fit in well at school and later acknowledged that he tended to be a "loner" (someone who does not make friends easily).

(7) In high school, Jobs worked on light displays for jazz programs and was involved with some film productions. In his senior year, he was making frequent visits to the University of California and to Stanford.

(8) In 1972 Steve Jobs graduated from high school and began college (university) at Reed College in Oregon. He soon dropped out to take a job at Atari, the computer game company.

(9) In 1974 Jobs, who was interested in eastern spirituality, visited India for seven months with friends. When he returned, he lived in a commune briefly where he became a practicing Zen Buddhist.

(10) Steve Jobs' older boyhood friend, Steve Wozniak redesigned the "Pong" and "Breakout" video games for Atari. Jobs followed Wozniak to Atari.

(11) Jobs, Wozniak, and another friend formed the Apple Computer Company in 1976.

(12) The first Apple Macintosh computer was introduced in 1984.

(13) In 1983 John Sculley had become CEO of Apple. He fell into conflict with Jobs when sales of the Macintosh were less than expected. Sculley reorganized Apple in 1985, and a displeased Jobs resigned from the company at that point.

(14) After leaving Apple, Jobs first founded the NeXT computer company. Then he invested in Pixar, the company which would lead the way in full length, animated films, partnering with

[92] Repo man: someone who repossesses automobiles for the lending institutions when borrowers fall too far behind on payments.

Disney Studios. Jobs eventually sold Pixar to Disney and took a seat on Disney's board of directors.

(15) In 1997 Apple purchased NeXT Computers and rehired Jobs as CEO. Apple was struggling at the time. Under Jobs' new leadership Apple introduced the iPod, iPhone, and iPad. Apple went from near extinction to a position of dominance in the market again.

(16) In 2003 Steve Jobs was diagnosed with cancer. He first tried to combat it with alternative medicines. A few years later he had a pancreatic transplant. He died in 2011.

Quotes from Steve Jobs

Your time is limited, so don't waste it living someone else's life. Don't be trapped by dogma - which is living with the results of other people's thinking. Don't let the noise of others' opinions drown out your own inner voice. And most important, have the courage to follow your heart and intuition.

Innovation distinguishes between a leader and a follower.

It's really clear that the most precious resource we all have is time.

Computers themselves, and software yet to be developed, will revolutionize the way we learn.

It's not a faith in technology. It's faith in people.

Oprah Winfrey (1954-present), O! Oprah!

(1) Oprah Winfrey was born in poverty to a single, teenage mother in rural Mississippi in 1954.

(2) Oprah was sexually molested at the age of 9 and became pregnant at the age of 14.

(3) During high school in Nashville, Tennessee, Oprah Winfrey was an honor student, member of the speech team, and voted "Most Popular Girl."

(4) At age 17 Oprah Winfrey won the Miss Black Tennessee beauty contest and got a job as a radio news announcer while in high school.

(5) At the age of 19, Winfrey was reporting television news and hosting a talk show in Chicago, Illinois.

(6) Oprah Winfrey went to college (university) on a full scholarship and studied journalism.

(7) Winfrey worked as a television news anchor in Nashville, Tennessee and Baltimore, Maryland before co-hosting a talk show in Baltimore in 1978.

(8) From 1986 through 2001, Oprah hosted a nationally televised talk show which was hugely popular. She elevated the topics and discussion with the goal of contributing something of value to the lives of her viewers. Her show was watched all over the world and she has had a significant impact on thought everywhere.

(9) Winfrey co-founded the women's cable television network, Oxygen, her own television production company, Harpo Productions, and her own magazine "O Magazine." All three of these endeavors have been successful.

(10) In 1985 Oprah Winfrey was featured in the acclaimed movie, *The Color Purple*, and was nominated for an Academy Award.

(11) In 1998 Winfrey produced and starred in *Beloved*, a film adaptation of Toni Morrison's Pulitzer Prize winning novel. Oprah has also acted in many other movies.

(12) Oprah Winfrey has co-authored 5 books.

(13) Oprah Winfrey is among the richest people in the world and is also considered to be one of the most influential people in the world.

(14) Winfrey has honorary doctoral degrees from Harvard and Duke.

(15) Winfrey was awarded the Presidential Medal of Freedom in 2013.

(16) Oprah Winfrey is among the world's leading philanthropists. She has given away hundreds of millions of dollars to a variety of causes.

(17) Winfrey is so well known that she is known instantly by her first name, Oprah.

Quotes from Oprah Winfrey

The more you praise and celebrate your life, the more there is in life to celebrate.

Think like a queen. A queen is not afraid to fail. Failure is another steppingstone to greatness.

The biggest adventure you can take is to live the life of your dreams.

Real integrity is doing the right thing, knowing that nobody's going to know whether you did it or not.

Surround yourself with only people who are going to lift you higher.

Passion is energy. Feel the power that comes from focusing on what excites you. The greatest discovery of all time is that a person can change his future by merely changing his attitude.

Excellence is the best deterrent to racism or sexism.

Where there is no struggle, there is no strength.

The struggle of my life created empathy - I could relate to pain, being abandoned, having people not love me.

I feel that luck is preparation meeting opportunity.

I have a lot of things to prove to myself. One is that I can live my life fearlessly.

Doing the best at this moment puts you in the best place for the next moment.

Turn your wounds into wisdom.

What I know is that if you do work that you love, and the work fulfills you, the rest will come.

It does not matter how you came into the world, what matters is that you are here.

Stephen Spielberg (1946-present) and American Films

(1) Stephen Spielberg was born to an orthodox Jewish family in Cincinnati, Ohio. Before Stephen finished school the family moved first to New Jersey, then to Phoenix, Arizona, then to Saratoga, California.

(2) As a small child, Stephen Spielberg experienced bullying, often related to the family's religious beliefs.

(3) Spielberg started making amateur films at the age of 12.

(4) At the age of 13, Spielberg won a prize for a 40 minute film he produced using classmates as actors.

(5) At the age of 16 Spielberg produced his first full length motion picture for $500.

(6) Stephen Spielberg was a serious Boy Scout. He achieved the highest scout rank, Eagle Scout.

(7) Stephen's parents divorced shortly before he finished high school.

(8) Spielberg attended California State University-Long Beach briefly. While there, he accepted an unpaid internship with Universal Studios. As an intern, he produced a short film which impressed studio executives. He was then offered a seven year contract to produce films for Universal.

(9) Spielberg's first big directorial success was *Jaws,* starring Richard Dreyfuss. The movie made him famous and a millionaire.

(10) Spielberg's second big hit movie was *Close Encounters of the Third Kind,* which he wrote and directed. Richard Dreyfuss, who had starred in *Jaws,* got the starring role in *Close Encounters.*

(11) Famous Spielberg films are many. They include the *Indiana Jones* movies; *Saving Private Ryan; Schindler's List; E.T., the Extra-terrestrial;*

The Color Purple; Empire of the Sun; Jurassic Park; Gremlins; Poltergeist; and *Amistad.*

(12) Spielberg won the Academy Award for best director twice—for *Schindler's List* and for *Saving Private Ryan.*

(13) *Schindler's List* won the Academy Award for best picture.

(14) In 1994 Stephen Spielberg co-founded DreamWorks Pictures.

(15) In 1995 Spielberg was awarded the American Film Institute's Lifetime Achievement Award.

(16) Spielberg's movies have made him a billionaire, and he has been a major contributor to the worldwide dominance of American film.

Quotes from Stephen Spielberg

The delicate balance of mentoring someone is not creating them in your own image, but giving them the opportunity to create themselves.

When I felt like an outsider, movies made me feel inside my own skill set.

Fathering is a major job, but I need both things in my life: my job to be a director, and my kids to direct me.

Mark Zuckerberg (1984-present), the Face of Social Media

(1) Mark Zuckerberg was the leading co-founder of Facebook. He currently is the CEO and board chairman of Facebook.

(2) Mark Zuckerberg was born in White Plains, New York in 1984, the son of a dentist and a psychiatrist.

(3) Zuckerberg attended college preparatory high schools. He was an excellent student with special interest in languages, sciences, and computers. He took advance college classes in computer programming while in high school. He was also captain of the fencing team.

(4) Zuckerberg created Facebook for Harvard students while attending Harvard. The growth and success of Facebook led him to drop out of Harvard.

(5) The number of people with Facebook accounts today is approximately 2 billion. (There are just over 7 billion people in the world.)

(6) The effects of Facebook on society and popular culture are mixed. On the negative side, Facebook participation is like an addiction for many people, especially the young, and Facebook is known to have been used to circulate false information widely. Zuckerberg's organization has yet to take any strong action to mitigate the problems.[93]

(7) On December 9, 2010, Zuckerberg, Bill Gates, and Warren Buffett signed a promise they called "The Giving Pledge", by which they promised to donate to charity at least half of their wealth and challenged all other super-wealthy people to do the same.

(8) Zuckerberg's charitable donations up to now have totaled approximately $1 billion.

Quotes from Mark Zuckerberg

The biggest risk is not taking any risk... In a world that changes really quickly, the only strategy that is guaranteed to fail is not taking risks.

Move fast and break things. Unless you are breaking stuff, you are not moving fast enough.

I think a simple rule of business is, if you do the things that are easier first, then you can actually make a lot of progress.

I think that more flow of information, the ability to stay connected to more people makes people more effective as people.

---

[93] Mitigate: to make less severe.

Ellen DeGeneres (1958-present), More than OK

(1) Ellen DeGeneres was born in Louisiana in 1958 to middle class professional parents. Her parents were divorced when she was 13. She moved to Atlanta, Georgia with her mother and sister when her mother remarried.

(2) DeGeneres attended the University of New Orleans for one semester in 1976.

(3) DeGeneres began doing stand-up comedy at clubs in New Orleans in 1981.

(4) DeGeneres did stand-up comedy on tour during the 1980s. Her big break was her first appearance on *The Tonight Show with Johnny Carson* in 1986.

(5) DeGeneres starred in the popular situation comedy *Ellen* from 1994 through 1998.

(6) Ellen DeGeneres announced to the world that she is gay (homosexual) on the *Oprah Winfrey Show* in 1997. Shortly after that, her character "Ellen" in her sitcom discussed her sexual orientation with a psychiatrist played by Winfrey. The admission and embrace of her sexual orientation openly was a brave and pioneering move at that time.

(7) The larger message is that it is okay. Sexual orientation is part of who we are, but who we are is much bigger; and sexual orientation is a personal thing—one's own business. Since 2003 Ellen DeGeneres has been hosting her own popular talk show. It is a celebration of humanity and women's empowerment and uplifting in the style of the Oprah Winfrey model.

(8) Ellen DeGeneres has hosted the Oscars (films), the Grammys (music), and the Day Time Emmys (television).

(9) In 2008, DeGeneres married actress Portia de Rossi.

(10) DeGeneres is the author of three books.

(11) DeGeneres founded her own record company in 2010 to give a voice to lesser known artists.

(12) DeGeneres has won 13 Emmys and 14 Peoples' Choice Awards.

(13) Ellen DeGeneres is the voice of Dory in the Pixar movie *Finding Nemo*.

(14) Ellen DeGeneres is a vegan and a committed advocate of animal rights.[94]

Quotes from Ellen DeGeneres

We focus so much on our differences, and that is creating, I think, a lot of chaos and negativity and bullying in the world.

Most comedy is based on getting a laugh at somebody else's expense. And I find that that's just a form of bullying in a major way. So I want to be an example that you can be funny and be kind, and make people laugh without hurting somebody else's feelings.

Here are the values that I stand for: honesty, equality, kindness, compassion, treating people the way you want to be treated and helping those in need. To me, those are traditional values.

Sometimes you can't see yourself clearly until you see yourself through the eyes of others.

I'm not an activist; I don't look for controversy. I'm not a political person, but I'm a person with compassion. I care passionately about equal rights. I care about human rights. I care about animal rights.

Find out who you are and be that person. That's what your soul was put on this Earth to be. Find that truth, live that truth and everything else will come.

It's our challenges and obstacles that give us layers of depth and make us interesting. Are they fun when they happen? No. But they are what make us unique. And that's what I know for sure... I think.

We need more kindness, more compassion, more joy, more laughter. I definitely want to contribute to that.

I learned compassion from being discriminated against. Everything bad that's ever happened to me has taught me compassion.

---

[94] Vegan: a person who does not eat meat or any animal products.

Printed in the United States
By Bookmasters